Essential

Florence

THE PRACTICAL GUIDE FOR LIVING IN FLORENCE

Nita Tucker *&* Victoria Miachika

ISBN: 145375783X
ISBN-13: 9781453757833

Table of Contents

Forward *vii*

1 **Before You Leave**
Where to live? 1
Finding a Home 5
The Paperwork 11
Preparing for Departure 14
Arriving 21

2 **A Room With A View And A Computer**
Codici Fiscali and Contracts xx
Utilities 25
Telephone and Internet 27
Cleaning, Garbage and Laundry 38

3 **Schools and Activities for Kids**
International Schools 43
Italian Schools and Curriculum 48
Activities for Kids 49
Teenagers and Cultural Challenges 56

4 **Work and Play**
Work 59
Social Life 61
Entertainment 67
Religion 78

5 To Market

Groceries and Staples   80
Markets   80
Household Goods   85
Outlet Shops   87

6 Getting Around

Public Transportation   95
Cars   99
Trains   106
Air Travel   108

7 Health and Well-Being

Emergency Numbers   xxx
Doctors and Pharmacies   xxx
Hospitals   xxx
Staying Fit   xxx

8 Day Trips (Traveler not Tourist)

Experiencing Florence and Tuscany   xxx

9 Daily Management Mantras

Embracing Cultural Differences   133
The Do's and Don'ts of Living Abroad   137
Useful Tips   143

10 Resources

Suggested Reading   145
Useful Websites   147

11 The Essential White Pages

Emergency Numbers	153
Other useful #'s	153
Calendar of Public Holidays	156
Weather: Average monthly temperatures	157
Telephone references	157
Home Sweet Home	159
Help Sweet Help (professional services and more)	160
Going Places	166
Healthy & Wise	168
For lovers of leisure	174
Where shopping begins	182
Sending your love	185
School Days	186
Museums, Galleries and Monuments	192
Embassies and Consulates	208

FORWARD

There is the romantic idea of living in Italy and then there is the daily reality. The two are not to be confused. With the recent popularity of such books as *Eat Pray Love* and *Under the Tuscan Sun*, a temporary home in Italy has become the romantic dream for many. Florence is a wonderful destination for such a venture. Rich in history, culture, food and wine, this small gem of a city is one of the most visited places in the world. For the long term 'traveler' its accessible size and history of hosting foreigners make it an ideal venue for a year or more abroad.

However fascinating the experience of exploring its culture and traditions prove to be, the daily practicalities of living in Florence present many challenges for the English-speaking foreigner. **Essential Florence** is a manual filled with practical and pragmatic information on how to arrive, survive and thrive in Florence. Intended for the Anglophone foreigner who plans to stay for more than a couple of weeks this book directs the reader to appropriate resources and services and helps avoid common and frustrating cultural pitfalls. Although this manual is about living in or near Florence many of the topics discussed are applicable to any Italian destination.

The Essential White Pages is a list of local services and resources, gathered with an English-speaking expat in mind.

Enjoy your adventure!
Victoria Miachika and Nita Tucker

A NOTE

This manual is a 'work in progress', and your feedback, updates, and additional information are welcome for future editions. Note that the opinions and referenced Italian cultural norms are based on personal experiences while living as a foreigner in Italy and are not presented as fact. Also, we apologize that the book is written using North America as the reference point, rather than representing our full Anglophone readership. This is a weakness we hope to correct in later editions. The information in the White Pages is intended to be a helpful starting point, and by no means should it be considered comprehensive. Finally, because time has a way of changing things, even in a city as old as Florence, we apologize in advance for any misinformation or misrepresentation.

*Please send your comments, additions, suggestions and corrections to: **info@essentialflorentine.com**.*

*"You may have the universe
if I may have Italy."
— Guissepe Verde*

1 BEFORE YOU LEAVE

Where to live?

Do you want to live in the heart of a suburban town or on its outskirts—near small villages and within easy driving distance to major cities? Does a central apartment in a historic building sound more suitable? What are your requirements for work, social life, or schools?

Where and 'how' you chose to live will greatly affect your experience abroad. Be clear about your expectations and needs before selecting your destination and accommodations. Make a list and evaluate each item in terms of its relevance and importance against your ultimate objective.

To help narrow down your choices, consider some of the following questions:

What are my interests?
(New people/ art/ food/ wine/ history/ nightlife)

What do I see myself doing every day?
(Working/ studying/ visiting cultural attractions/ shopping/ farming/
learning the language/ food/ wine/ art)

How do I see myself living?
(Driving/ walking/ house/ apartment/ social interactions)

Answering these sorts of questions will help define expectations and ultimately assist you in making appropriate decisions about where to live as well as clarify requirements for suitable accommodation. Listed beow are some pros and cons to consider when choosing either city or the countryside.

CITY LIVING

Pros

- *Wide range of activities (cultural, shopping, educational)*
- *Locals more familiar with foreigners and cultural diversity*

- Easier access to English-speaking support (business and social)
- Services (schools, courses, medical and professional)
- Many stores and suppliers; wide selection of goods
- Easy travel options and international access (trains/ airports/ highways)

Cons

- Busy, crowded
- Higher cost of living
- Less living space, usually older apartment buildings with little access to greenery
- High levels of tourism sometimes causes locals to be less friendly toward foreigners
- People tend to speak English, making it more difficult to learn Italian and local customs
- Parking a car is difficult
- Extremely hot in peak summer months

SMALLER TOWNS OR COUNTRYSIDE

Pros

- Quiet, usually fewer foreigners
- Increased opportunities to meet locals and learn traditions and language
- Accommodation is generally cheaper, with access to gardens and terraces
- Parking and car ownership is less of a hassle
- Less hot in summer months

Cons

- Limited access to a variety of services and products
- Fewer people able to communicate in English
- Accommodation may have operational challenges and require more servicing(gardens/pools/ gates)

- *More difficult to access some of the cultural treasures of Italy*
- *Travel on country roads during winter and peak tourist months may be difficult*
- *Sometimes feels a bit isolated*

Finding a Home

Rentals can be short-term, long-term, fully furnished or completely unfurnished. An abundance of agencies for short-term rentals (under two months) cater primarily to the tourist trade or students. Longer-term rentals or purchases usually require an agent.

The Internet is a good starting point to get an overview of the broad range of accommodation options available in Florence and the surrounding region. Searches will yield listings of agents, private owners, hoteliers, shared accommodations, exchange opportunities and countless other choices. In this book, **The Essential White Pages** includes a list of resources and contacts to help you find agents, agencies and other useful services.

Local newspapers are always a good source for scouting out housing opportunities. The English-speaking newspaper in Florence, *The Florentine*, is published bi-weekly, is free in print and online ***www.florentine.net***. The classifieds section usually has notices for houses and apartments for rent or sale as well as adverts for qualified agencies specializing in relocation and accommodation.

Foreign schools, universities or national consulates near your Italian destination can be excellent resources for local housing suggestions. The Internet will bring up a long list of English-speaking schools and consular corps in Italy. Try contacting their administration or receptionist for possible lists of available rentals or recommendations for a good local agency. The Italian embassy, consulate or cultural centers in your own home towns may also be willing to provide information on housing in Italy. Another useful source is the well-known Craigs List, which recently added a Florence site: ***www.florence.craigslist.com***.

Buying a home: If you are considering buying a home, it's best to work with an agent and lawyer. There are several

English-speaking agencies that specialize in Italian properties (see The *Essential Florentine White Pages*). If you have never lived in Italy and are unfamiliar with the market, you may want to consider renting first. This is a safe way to familiarize your self with different opportunities and the daily rituals of a particular neighborhood or area.

Working with an Agent or Agency

Real estate agents in Italy who deal in sales or long-term rentals will be familiar with all necessary paperwork and procedures. Agencies tend to charge a fee of approximately 10 percent of the total rental contract or a one-month rental fee for terms of less than a year. Note that a fee is paid by **both** parties, the landlord and the tenant. Though working with an agent is a more expensive option, keep in mind the service generally includes negotiating terms, overseeing legal concerns about renting or buying and other relocation services. The agent will remain a valuable source of information and support during your tenancy. Some agents will also help you acquire a *codice fiscale*, the tax number required for you to draw up contracts in Italy.

You can work with agents long distance by Internet or phone, but it's recommended that you make at least one visit to your potential accommodation before you sign any contracts or pay deposits.

Contracts

A contract between landlord and lessee is best negotiated with the help of an agent, a lawyer, (*avvocato*) or accountant (*commercialista*). The agent is responsible for ensuring that all legal necessities are appropriately addressed. If you are renting, remember to be clear about what is included in the rent. Outline your expectations and negotiate your needs prior to arrival. Utilities usually cost extra and there is often a fee for upkeep of the building's communal areas or the presence of a concierge. Discuss whether you are taking over the utilities from a previous renter/owner, *subentro*, or transferring all bills to your name, *voltura*. Ask about Internet, phone connections and television hook-up. These are not standard features in Italy and they often require additional organization.

Un-registered lease: In Italy, it is common to find landlords willing to receive part or all of the rent under the table, *pagare in nero*. Cash payments allow landlords to claim less income and thus avoid paying taxes on the money they receive. Renters who pay in cash should expect reduced rent. Although people frequently rent without a registered lease, **it is not legal**, and tenants have no official contract upon which to take recourse should things not go according to pre-established expectations or verbal agreements. Choose according to your own level of comfort and remember it's okay to negotiate; it is the Italian way.

Things to consider when looking for a home in the city

Neighborhood. Before your final decision make sure you understand the neighborhood. Your choice of neighborhood will affect your access to staples and ultimately influence the daily cost of living. Is the neighborhood primarily residential, tourist or commercial? Are there restaurants, bars and small grocery shops nearby? What kind of people live there? Are there any locals or is it mostly an area for hotels and businesses? Grocery shops in more tourist areas are more expensive and carry less selection. How can you access services and do you need transportaion. In prime areas of the historic city center a car is not a necessity and you have the advantage of easy access to sites and attractions.

Noise. Some locations may *look* idyllic, but apartments located in major piazzas or homes overlooking the Arno can *sound* like you're living in the middle of a construction site or nightclub. Traffic, especially the incessant buzz of *motorini*, scooters, can be disruptive. If you can't forsake the view check for double-paned windows. Also, if it is likely to bother you, make sure that there are no blue garbage dumpsters directly below your windows. They are emptied in the wee hours of the morning and are notoriously noisy.

Stairs. Accommodation with more than three flights of stairs and no elevator can prove a chore when transport-ing groceries, luggage or furniture. Rent will often reflect the presence of an elevator. Note that when you request home delivery, suppliers often ask what floor you live on and if your building has an elevator; having no elevator generally implies that an extra surcharge will be added to your delivery bill.

Telephone/Computer. Ensure you have adequate outlets for the phone and Internet. Some of the older buildings may be a bit of a challenge and require updating. Check with the landlord about the status of the phone and Internet accessibility before you sign a lease. Getting something organized after the deal may prove difficult.

Note: your landlord may assure you that there is com-puter access in the apartment, but this can mean dif-ferent things. More often than not, it means 'dial-up'.

High-speed access with ADSL requires specific wiring. Make sure these details are handled BEFORE you arrive in Italy. Hundreds of ex-pat horror stories involve applying for ADSL. Many landlords and agents say that hook-up will be no problem and suggest you sign up for it yourself when you arrive; the 'wait' can last anywhere from two months to three years.

Washer and Dryers. Florentine apartments rarely have both a washer and a dryer as space is limited and the cost of running a dryer is very high. Most accommodations provide only a washing machine and an assortment of clothes-lines for drying. Known for producing sky-high electric bills, combined 'washer/dryers' are sometimes available but they only allow for small loads.

Air conditioning. Though air conditioning is expensive to operate life can become unbearable in the summer months without it. Some apartments located on the lower floors of old stone buildings do not become quite as hot as do the upper floors. Check the windows of your apartment to see that they have good shutters to block out the heat in summer and the cold in the winter especially when you are looking at single pane older glass.

Parking. Not many city accommodations include parking for either cars or bikes, so check street availability. Public garages offer daily and monthly rates but have limited hours and tend to be quite costly. Monthly rental rates vary according to the size of your car; bigger cars call for higher fees.

Terraces and balconies. These are lovely city amenities and you are likely to pay extra for them. Sadly the summer heat, noise and mosquitoes often negate the benefits of a sunny terrace in the city center. Note that BBQ's are not allowed on patios or terraces in Florence.

9

Fireplaces. Unless they are gas fireplaces are usually only decorative. Ask if your fireplace is usable. If not make sure it's sealed or you will curse the cold air during the winter months. .

Swimming pools. Pools are considered a luxury and can sometimes be found outside of Florence in larger villa complexes. As a wonderful summer amenity, they may require payment of a monthly maintenance fee. In complexes where there are several homes sharing a pool, you may encounter certain usage restrictions as well. Make sure you understand the rules/costs of using and maintaining a pool. City-dwellers can use public pools near the center and join swim clubs at reasonable rates.

Mosquitoes. Florence and the countryside are notorious in the summer for pesky mosquitoes. Numerous products are available in the shops, such as plug-in insecticides (*Vape*) or innovative contraptions that electronically zap mosquitoes. Citronella lanterns can make leaving your windows open at night bearable. Better yet look for an apartment that has screens on the windows. At hardware stores you can find 'screen' material to tape over the windows or mosquito netting to be hung over the beds at night. Consider having your terraces and gardens sprayed.

The Paperwork

The legal paperwork necessary for moving to Italy depends largely on *the reason behind your move*. If you are re-locating for work or study you will require a specific visa. Ask your school or employer for assistance in providing necessary documents. Proof of employment is mandatory in order to obtain a working visa and a student visa requires certification that you are enrolled in an accredited course.

NOTE: REQUIREMENTS FOR VISAS CHANGE REGULARLY. WORK DIRECTLY WITH YOUR LOCAL ITALIAN EMBASSY/ CONSULATE FOR CURRENT REQUIREMENTS, FORMS, AND FEES.

Whether your time abroad is for work or personal pleasure, you will need a visa for stays over three months. There are many different kinds of visas, including a residency visa, which is generally granted to individuals with proof of an annual income. Contact the Italian embassy or consulate nearest you. Most preliminary inquiries can be done through the Internet. The embassy and consulate websites outline the different types of visa available and their corresponding requirements. You may be asked to submit proof of a clean criminal record and certify that you have ample funds to live in the country without becoming a burden to the Italian taxpayer.

Possible visa requirements
Valid passport
Criminal record check
Proof of funds: copies of financial statements/income.
Medical insurance

A letter stating why you are going to Italy, where you will be living, who you are traveling with and how long you plan to stay.
Proof of your residency in the city where you are applying
A round-trip ticket

Anticipate paperwork after you arrive in Florence

PERMESSO DI SOGGIORNO (Permission to stay)
Once visa holders land on Italian soil, they have a limited number of days (usually eight) to register with the local police or *Questura*. Once registered at the *Questura*, you must request a *permesso di soggiorno*. This is a legal document stating you have permission to stay in Italy for more than three months. To apply for a *permesso di soggiorno*, go to the main post office in Florence's Piazza della Repubblica and request a complete application package. Once you have filled out all the paperwork, take the required documentation and two photos to the *Questura* office.

Standard requirements
Copy of your passport with proof of a valid visa
Two passport photos
Two official stamps (*bolli*), available at any *tabaccheria* shop
Copies of the documentation you needed for your visa

CODICE FISCALE (Tax-Code Number)
Even though you may not be subject to Italian taxes, it is obligatory for all citizens, whether Italian or foreign nationals, to have a *codice fiscale*. This code is necessary for any of the following:

Opening a bank or postal account
Buying or leasing a motor vehicle
Signing any official contract (rent, cell phone, etc.)
Taking any sort of employment
Signing contracts to engage utility services

A *codice fiscale* is easy to acquire and all you need is a valid passport. Some agents or landlords will apply for one for you prior to arrival since you need to have the code before you can sign a rental agreement. If you arrive in Italy without one, see Chapter 2 for more details and check the website: www.agenziaentrate.it.

DO I REALLY NEED THE PAPERWORK?
There are numerous ex-pats living comfortably (but illegally) in Italy with neither a visa nor a *permesso*. Although it is cumbersome to get the paperwork together, you will certainly benefit from a legally recognized, stamped EEC visa in your passport. The visa makes travel between continents worry-free and gives you access to Italian government services, banking, permits and medical services.

Preparing for Departure

Armed with your valid passport and a contracted living space in Italy, you are ready to plan your departure. Here is a short list of some things to take care of before leaving:

Medical. Schedule routine medical, dental appointments and examinations before departure. Speak with your team of physicians to let them know of your travel plans and ask for copies of your medical records, prescriptions or important x-rays (dental x-rays, mammograms, etc.). Make sure you know your blood type and that of those traveling with you. Have your doctor's contact information as well as a list of medical experts who can be reached in case of an emergency. Ask your insurance company for details about your coverage and find out how to get reimbursed for medical services while in Italy.

Bank. Let your bank know that you are traveling outside the country for a lengthy period of time and may require them to wire funds to an Italian account. You might want to arrange a Power of Attorney in case of emergency banking/deposit box needs. Make sure your bankcard can access international automatic tellers. Verify that your account is current and that all your passwords function properly. Passwords often need to be modified to insure they have the right number of digits for ATM machines in Italy.

Credit cards. Notify all of your major credit card companies regarding your travel itinerary so there are no disruptions to service.

Lawyers. Make sure you have an up-to-date will to leave with your lawyer or in a safety deposit box at your bank.

Organize a Power of Attorney for any emergency or business/financial needs.

Insurance. Take care of any travel and health insurance needs. Review coverage of personal goods and home insurance while traveling. Have policy copies to take with you and leave them along with other important personal documents in a bank deposit box or other secure location.

Post Office. Complete a change of address form if necessary and/or organize for your mail to be sent to a PO box where friends or relatives can easily retrieve it and forward to you later.

International Driver's License. Though not necessarily required it's easy to get and useful to have in addition to your national driver's license.

Shipping. If you are shipping goods to your new home, allow ample time for your packages to arrive. Check all requirements regarding insurance and delivery. Will the shipping company deliver directly to your new address, or will your belongings be taken to a warehouse, where you'll have to arrange pick-up and delivery yourself? Make sure you take all necessary documents, packing slips and contact numbers for both the shipper and receiver. The cost of shipping does not include custom fees which are calculated and charged once you receive the goods in Italy.

Cells and computers: Before leaving, check whether your cell phone can accommodate a European SIM card. (Many Blackberry/Treos need to be 'unlocked'. This is a US feature, so the system has to be unlocked before you leave for Italy.) You can then switch the card with a European sim card upon your arrival, eliminating the need to buy or rent a new phone. If your phone has roaming capabilities, call your provider and ensure the number permits access to European providers. Bring appropriate adapters for your phone and computer in order to accommodate 220V. Buying or renting a cell phone in Italy is very easy, quick and cost efficient (see Chapter 2). If, however, you prefer to arrange a cell phone rental prior to leaving, try ***www.piccellwireless.com*** or call (206) 780-0478.

Cars. If you are planning on purchasing a car or leasing one for an extended period of time, it's best to organize before you arrive in Italy. See Chapter 6.

Reading Helps Prepare the Way
Living in today's global world requires information. All too often, poor judgment, prejudices and failure are simply the result of the lack of understanding. Take time to learn about the country you're moving to. It's a small investment of time considering how much your acquired knowledge will contribute to making your stay in Italy a successful, life-enriching experience. See Chapter 10 for a list of some suggested 'good reads' about Florence, the region, and Italy. Learn about the country's current political situation, dominant religion and cultural values. What are the people like? Who are their heroes? What is their history? The more knowledge you bring with you to the Italian table, the more you'll enjoy the feast.

Top 10 things you NEED to know: That Italians assume you already DO know, SHOULD know and are stupid for NOT knowing!

#10 Hours: *The rule about scheduled hours is that there is absolutely no rule. However, some of the following 'customs' may or may not apply. And from whatever anyone tells you, no matter if it is the official website, the mayor, the owner of the store, or a government decree, you can always add the words, 'usually except not always'.*

On Mondays, many stores are either closed or don't open until after 2:30pm. Restaurants often are closed on Mondays or Tuesdays, and some just open for dinner or just for lunch. One of my favorites only closes on Saturday. Some stores, usually those in the centre, have continual hours—This means they don't close for the afternoon 'siesta'. When a store re-opens is anybody's guess. Some open their doors at 4:00, 4:30 or 5:30—or not at all. The last place you usually will find a business' schedule is from a sign posted on the door. There are many of these signs but they are not usually filled in. The supermarkets are usually closed on Sundays, except for the last Sunday of the month.

The wonderful antique and flea markets around Italy have a similar way of scheduling. Arezzo has it's famous antique market on the first weekend of the month (on Saturday and Sunday). But if the 1st falls on a Sunday, then it's still considered the first weekend.

Regarding museum hours, I have concluded that the creativity that was used to make the amazing art housed in these museums is now applied to the scheduling. I recently read a xeroxed sign at the Medici Chapel—a frequently visited state museum. The schedule went something like this: 'Open every 3rd Monday in summers from 11:30-1:30 except for August. Tuesdays and Thursdays from 9-5pm, Friday afternoons in winter.' The weekends had different hours every 2nd weekend depending on when the Uffizzi was open. And this wasn't a joke!!

I asked the concierge of a major hotel to check the Sunday hours for the Prada Outlet. He checked the website and it said that the outlet was closed on Sunday. I knew it was open, but he kept pointing to the website. So I asked him to call, he grudgingly agreed, and, of course, it was open. It's always open on Sunday, everyone knows that—only their own website was uninformed.

#9 *Wash and Dry: If you rent an apartment with a washing machine, be prepared to wait hours for a wash. Most machines take two hours— then you have to hang it on the line to dry because dryers are scarce.*

#8 *Strike! At any time and for whatever reason (or without reason) there may be a 'sciopero' , the Italian word for 'strike'. I once had to take a train to Rome, and I was told that although there would be a strike, a few trains would still be running. I went to the station, the train was on the board, and then 5 minutes before the train was due to go, the word 'sorpresso' was displayed. This means 'suppressed' and it also meant, 'We got you, too'.*

#7 *Taxis: You watch the fare and get your money out as you drive up to your destination, then you look up and the driver has pushed 'the button'. The meter which had been 8.95 euro two seconds before, now reads, 11.50 euro. This is because*
   a. *You called the taxi, which deserves an added charge.*
   b. *It's after 11pm. The 'evening fare' time can change depending on the season, day of the week, and whether you are a woman or man.*
   c. *You have gone or come from the airport or train station.*
   d. *An unexpected new tariff applies or*
   e. *All of the above.*

#6 *Hidden charges: If you drink your cappuccino at the bar, it costs one euro, if you drink it while sitting at a table (even if you bought it at the bar), it costs more, usually double. In some 'refined' places like Piazza Signoria or Piazza della Repubblica, you pay such an exorbitant amount for one cup of coffee, that you should be able to take the table home with you, too!*

#5 *Addresses: Street numbering in Florence follows the standard: 'even' numbers on one side of the street, 'odd' on the other. (Again, usually, except not always). But then there is the matter of the 'rosso'* or red numbers. The red numbers have very little to do sequentially with the black or blue numbers. So in your search for 32r, you might pass a black 30, and a black 34 and often even a black 32 which places you in front of a hotel when you are looking for a bike repair. (The bike repair you are looking for at 32r is two blocks further up next to a black 58).

#4 Driving: Once you are thoroughly stumped by numbers, you are ready to drive in Italy. My judgment is that Italians don't do signage well. For example, you are driving to Siena from Florence. You follow signs that get you into a roundabout. And you think it's simple—all you have to do is find the exit off of the roundabout with the sign to Siena. Except that five out of the six exits all have signs to Siena. Now, I don't have any advice on what to do, but I have discovered that the Italians don't seem to have any problem with this, the signs work just fine for them.

#3 Taking the train: You are in Florence, you want to go to the wonderful antique market in Arezzo, because it's the first weekend of the month. You go to the train station and buy a ticket to Arezzo. You are given a ticket that says Arezzo, the train number and the time. Then you look at the reader board to see which binario, track, your train is leaving from. Arezzo is not on the board. Rome is on the board, Milano is on the board, Palermo is on the board, but there's no Arezzo. You look at the number on your ticket again to see if it matches one of the bigger destinations, but no numbers except times are on the board. Then, of course you try to match times—but the trains for Milano and Roma leave at the same time. Finally, you ask a train employee, who looks at your ticket, the reader board, and then at you, because he can't believe he's met such an imbecile. Then he scolds you for wasting his time on such an idiotic question, because any fool knows that the train to Rome stops in Arezzo!!

#2 Tipping: Wait staff in Italy get paid wages and do not depend on tips. There is a charge in restaurants called 'coperto' which is added to the check and covers the cost of bread and service. Tipping is still appreciated, it just doesn't have to be a percentage of the bill, and is based on the quality of the service. Most taxis do not expect tips, but again, it doesn't hurt to be generous and kind.

And the **#1** thing you need to know, that every Italian knows, and thinks you're stupid for not knowing is: 'Sconto?' You can always ask, any one and anywhere for a discount. In the major stores or if you are buying a peach in the market (though I can't imagine why you would care about a discount on the peach). You do not need to ask for it like you are driving a tough bargain, but rather that you are asking for a gesture of friendship. And it is given in the same spirit. Enjoy!

Arriving

Plan to be agenda-free the first couple of days after your arrival so you can sleep off any jet-lag and slowly settle into your environment. Take the time to get comfortable in your new home and to familiarize yourself with its operational logistics. Ask your landlord/agent to give you details about the location, household maintenance and billing arrangements for any utilities. Make sure you understand how to use the phone, intercom, or Internet connections. Ask to be introduced to any neighbors who might be able to assist you with possible logistical problems. Does anyone nearby speak English? The secret to feeling comfortable in your new home is getting yourself oriented both physically and mentally.

Create a Neighborhood Resource List

Knowing where you live in relation to the larger surrounding area can help forge your sense of belonging. Begin assembling a list of services, people and businesses you might draw upon for future needs.

Get your bearings by wandering around your new neighborhood. Take note of street names, local coffee bars and shops. What type of area are you living in? Are there lots of attractions and stores or is it more residential? Where can you buy milk, fruit, your morning coffee, newspapers and aspirin? Locate nearby services and transportation links. Find out where you can get phone cards, buy bus tickets, use internet or make photocopies. Check out the nearest medical facility and locate ATM machines and hardware stores. Visit English-speaking bookstores, churches or information centers and ask about possible groups/clubs to meet or join. Locate government offices (both national and foreign), the post office, the police station, schools and libraries as well as local community programs and activity centers.

Pick up The Florentine at a bookstore or consulate, or come right to our office at:
The Florentine
Via dei Banchi 4
50123 Firenze
055 230 6616
www.theflorentine.net

"We must be willing to let go of the life we have planned, so as to have the life that is waiting for us."

— E.M. Forster

2 A ROOM WITH A VIEW AND A COMPUTER

Managing your new home requires contracting utilities, sourcing trades, paying bills and acquiring the essentials of communication and entertainment.

Note about language: Contacting utility companies for non-Italian speakers can be stressful and many times might require assistance. However, it is worth an effort to make an initial call yourself, as you may find someone who does speak some English. Following is a 'script' of how a conversation might take place:

The phone answers and you say: Buon giorno. Mi scusi ma non parlo italiano, parla inglese? Often the answer will be, 'Yes, a little.' Or the person will find someone who can help you. Then, continue your conversation in English, speaking slowly and clearly. Remember to thank them for speaking in English and be sure to compliment them for how good their English is – even if it is not that great. If you can not communicate, then call back again when you have a friend or neighbor with you who can facilitate the translation.

Getting a *Codice Fiscale* (Tax-code number)

In order to enter into a contract of any kind you will require a *codice fiscale*. Your landlord or real estate agent may have already taken care of this for you or your landlord may have contracted services using his or her code, but it is best to have your own. It's relatively easy and quick to apply for a tax-code number.

Present yourself at the provincial tax office in Florence (*Ufficio imposte*) in via Santa Caterina D'Alessandria 23 (3rd floor) between the hours of 8:30am and 12pm. You will be required to show a valid passport and asked to fill out a simple form in exchange for a personalized code, which you can start using right away. The actual card will be mailed to your Italian address.

Utilities

Listed below are the major utility companies serving Florence and most of Tuscany. You can contact them by phone or via their websites.

GAS: Fiorentinagas
www.fiorentinagasclienti.it
For emergencies or sudden interruption of service: **800 862048**
Customer service toll free number: **800 509124**

ELECTRICITY: Enel
www.prontoenel.it
Toll free number: **800 900800** or dial **16441** in case of interruption of service.

Electricity is particularly expensive in Italy so be power-smart and remember to turn off all lights, air-conditioning units and heaters when not needed. Note that each household or property has an allotted amount of power available for use at any given time. Should you exceed your regulated quota, your main breakers will automatically switch off. Familiarize yourself with the location of the breakers, as it's common to suddenly lose electricity, especially when using more than two appliances simultaneously. If you run both a washing machine and a dishwasher at the same time, for example, it may cause power failure.

Converters: Italy uses 220V and requires converters (to convert 110 to 220) and/ or adapters for any electrical appliances from North America. Many new computers and cell phones do not need a converter, but it is vital to check first so as not to irreparably damage your equipment. Note that there are several socket sizes in Italy. You may require an adapter with various prong sizes to accommodate different appliances. Play it safe—buy a set of multiple adapters and keep them handy...it will alleviate a lot of frustration.

WATER SUPPLY: PubliAcqua Spa

Toll free number: **800 238238** or dial **800 314314** for technical difficulties.

You will be charged for water consumption and be aware that it's quite expensive. Enjoy long showers and baths but recognize that they are luxuries—even a short shower can cost up to 10 euro! A warning to you and your guests—avoid flushing feminine products or foreign objects down the toilet; the plumbing won't stand for it!

Telephone, Cellular & Internet

Landlines in Italy are costly with fees averaging approximately 30 euro per month whether or not you actually place calls. Landline packages generally include local calls to other landlines but expect to be charged when calling a cell phone or when phoning a city outside of the region, like Rome or Milan.

Warning: many ex-pats are shocked by the elevated cost of their phone bills. Calls to cell phones are usually the ones to blame for unpleasant surprises at the end of the pay period. Rule of thumb: Landline to landline, and cell phone to cell phone. (Exorbitant surcharges usually don't apply when calling from a cell phone to a landline).

For long distance calls to other countries, a good option is to buy a credit calling card to avoid expensive charges. Otherwise, consider purchasing one of the numerous value-packed international calling cards from a local *tabaccheria*. These cards come in various denominations and the instructions for use can be found on the back (see below). Make sure you ask for a card that works for your desired area, as some do not allow combined calls to North America or Australia. One of the better cards is the *Europa*. Unfortunately, calling cards cannot be used for dialing foreign toll free numbers.

NOTE: These calling cards are great if used from a landline to call abroad; they are not as economical when calling from a cell phone. For example, a 10-euro card will provide you with up to six hours of talking time from a home-based landline; however the same card allows only 40 minutes of credit when calling from a cell phone.

Instructions on How to Use a Calling Card
First, dial the 800 number listed on the back for English. Then, wait for the prompts that ask you for the secret

scratch-off code. After correctly inserting the code, you should dial the phone number you wish to reach. Remember to always dial 00 + country code + city code + number.

TELECOM ITALIA (*www.187.it*) is Italy's major phone provider offering basic phone lines as well as packages with ADSL.

Useful TELECOM Numbers:
For queries dial: 187
For technical difficulties: 182
For directory assistance: 176 (international) or 12 (national)
For information: 412 or dial 2 to speak directly to an operator
For remaining credit: 4612
For automatic redialing on a busy signal: 5

Other services:
There are growing numbers of telecommunication services available in Florence that offer excellent rates and programs for international calls.

SKYPE: Via a laptop or personal computer you can set up an internet account that is free of charge when speaking to another SKYPE user. For a nominal fee, users can also call regular landlines and cell phones. For subscriptions or additional information check out their website at: *www.skype.com*

VONAGE: If you have ADSL, then Vonage is one of the pioneers of VOIP technology, which, like Skype, allows you to place and receive calls internationally. For mere pennies, you can have a US or Canadian phone number that rings in Florence. You choose the area code and it costs the caller no more than if they were dialing from next door. With this system you can make unlimited calls to and from any cell phone or landline in the US, Canada, England, France, or Mexico for approx $25 a month. It requires a router and you need to be near your computer but the other caller can be on any type of phone. Advantages include being able to call 1-800 numbers. Check out their website at ***www.vonage.com***

MCI
Note that both MCI and Vonage may require some special equipment purchases.
www.mci.com.

The Telecom Italia Phone Center
Located at via Cavour 21r, this center is a useful spot where you can use public phones in case your cell or landline is down. In Florence, public phones are few and far between and they are seldom equipped to take coins. Most only accept electronic phone cards or, if lucky, credit cards. The TELECOM ITALIA PHONE CENTER provides private booths where you can use a phone card or pay cash after making all your calls. The center also has phone books for all of Europe and their clerks provide useful information about telephone services and phone cards. Landline or account assistance is also available.

Cell Phones

Over the past decade, the cell phone has truly become a universal essential appendage or adornment. Almost everyone in Italy has a cell phone and in residences, cell phones often replace landlines completely. You can either rent or buy one. It's also possible to bring one over from North America. Imported phones should either have roaming capability (convenient but very expensive) or allow you to change the SIM card to a European one. If you plan on staying in Florence for a substantial period of time, it's preferable to purchase a local sim card, as overseas services charge inflated rates to make local calls. Florence's two main providers of mobile service are VODAFONE and TIM. Both have outlets all over the city.

Buying a Cell and Phone Time

Cell phones can be bought from any household appliance shop (such as *Imperiale*) and/or large market stores. Cell phones normally come with a SIM card and a small amount of credit. In Italy you buy phone time ahead of using it, so there are no bills to deal with later. You can purchase credit at virtually any *tabaccheria*, newsstand, phone store or bar that sells *una ricarica*, or top up card. They come in various denominations. (Note: if you go over 11 months without topping up, your number will automatically be cancelled.)

It's very easy to top up a phone: just follow the directions on the back of the card and make sure you insert your correct cell phone number or else you risk buying time for someone else! You can also purchase phone credit directly from a TIM or VODAFONE outlet, though you may find yourself waiting in a lengthy line.

When buying a cell phone in Italy consider your needs carefully. Unless you require fancy upgrades buy a basic model so if something goes wrong you won't get too upset to discover that it can not be fixed because no one has access to any parts.

Two centrally located telephone shops are:

Spazio Omnitel - *via Panzani 33r, Santa Maria Novella. Tel: 055/2670121*

Il Telefonino (TIM) - *via Pelliceria 3. Tel: 055/2396066*

Renting A Phone

In order to rent a phone you'll need a credit card, an email address and a passport. Some Internet companies also rent cell phones. A couple of options within easy access of the city center are:

Internet Train - via Guelfa 24a. Tel: 055/214794 - *guelfa@fopm;ome/ot*

Cells4rent on via del'Oriolo 25r. Tel: 055/2345322 – www.cells4rent.com

USEFUL NUMBERS:

Overseas Dialing:
Dial 00 to get an overseas line, then the country code, followed by the city code. Finally, dial the local number you are calling. A listing of country and city codes can be found in the white pages under '*comunicazioni internazionali - prefissi internazionali*'.

Some common codes:

USA/ Canada	001
Australia	0061
England	0044

To dial within mainland Europe you only require the country code, area code and number.

Access Numbers:

AT&T:	800 172 444
MCI:	800 905 825 from a landline
	800 172 402 from a cell phone.
Telstra (Australia):	800 172 610.
To call collect:	172 1011
To speak to an English-speaking operator:	172 1012

Wake up service: Dial 4114. You'll be asked to input your desired wake up time based on a 24-hour clock. For example: if you want to be woken up at 6am, input 0600. Next, insert your phone number including the local area code (055 for Florence).

Note about Italian Phone Numbers:
Italian phone numbers can range anywhere from 2 digits to 11 or more. Within Italy all landlines begin with a 0. Italian cell phones begin with a 3.

Computers

As you would expect you will be able to use any computer in Italy, just make sure that it is compatible with 220V. European computers often have slight differences from their North American counterparts. To type the '@' sign for example, you use 'alt 2', or 'alt q'. Just make sure you ask which keys apply before you use or rent a computer.

Internet Access

There are several providers for ADSL which is the service you need for high-speed wireless connections. You can arrange this type of account with your phone provider—the largest company being Telecom Italia. Wireless is a latecomer to Italy and numerous suppliers are beginning to sprout up all over the city.

There are internet access points all over the city so you should never be stuck for somewhere to hook up and catch up on emails. Most companies charge 5 euro per hour and there are often discounts for students. Remember to bring an ID in order to register and use a computer in any of these spots. More and more bars and coffee shops are providing free Wi-FI access.

Internet Train via dei Benci 36r, Santa Croce (055/2638555) One of the first Internet chains in Italy, this company now has over 14 shops in Florence. Friendly English-speaking staff can help you with any queries.

Intotheweb via de Conti 23r, San Lorenzo (055/2645628) With over 18 computers and a helpful staff who speaks English, this company also rents cell phones, sells phone cards and sends and receives faxes.

Virtual Office via Faenza 49r, San Lorenzo (055/2645560) This internet establishment provides various related services such as Internet courses, international shipping and money transfers. They have DVD players and web-cams on some of their PC's.

Netgate via Sant Egidio 10r, Santa Croce (055/2347967) For more locations check their website at ***www.thenet-gate.it***

A number of Italian providers offer free Internet access:
Libero ***www.libero.it***
Tiscali ***www.tiscali.it***
Kataweb ***www.kataweb.com***
Telecom Italia ***www.tin.it***
Wind ***www.inwind.it***

Computer Assistance and Accessories

Getting a computer set up at home may require quite a bit of patience and possibly some local expertise. There are several companies and individuals in Florence who can help with house calls. Please check the *Essential Florence White Pages: Services* for current information.

Shops for accessories and support information:
Computer Discount Store, viale Matteotti 9
Data Port Macintosh, viale Guidoni 173
Intleco, via Dupre 11r
Tutto Computer, via del Giardino della Bizzarria 19 (Novoli Area)

Television

At the time of printing Italy has six major networks all of which are broadcast in Italian. Three of the networks are Berlusconi owned Mediaset channels. Generally speaking, there is very limited quality programming in Italy. Most channels focus on reality shows, game shows, singing festivals, live chat shows and some American dubbed re-runs. In addition, there are various local stations that feature a plethora of adverts and promotional programs. If you have youngsters, note that networks broadcast a fair amount of easily accessible soft porn.

You can supplement your basic TV package with digital satellite TV. Receivers and antennas are widely available in Italy, and you can use them to receive a diverse range of alternative programming. Some of these programs do require specific types of decoders. The satellite TV company SKY TV is one of the better subscription-based services. A provider that allows you to select original language (mostly English) soundtracks for non-Italian programming, **SKY** is part of the group belonging to Mr. Rupert Murdoch. SKY often promotes its special offers at television outlet stores and supermarkets.

In addition to SKY, there are other satellites that transmit throughout Europe. They can often be received free with a digital satellite receiver. **Hotbird, Astr and Eutelsat** tend to be oriented more towards Northern European programming. UK satellite decoders are also available. Check out SKY CARDS UK for access.

NOTE: Both Fastweb and Telecom have packages that include satellite TV, telephone and Internet (ADSL).

Paying Bills

Bills are mailed out approximately once every 2 months and payments are generally due 3 to 4 weeks after the date of issue. Unpaid bills usually warrant a warning note before services are disconnected. Do not count on one however, as disconnection can also occur without prior notice. Expect a reconnection fee of approximately 50 euro or more depending on the individual company and the reason the service was disconnected.

In Italy you cannot pay bills by mail. Consumers can choose one of the following payment options:

- *Cash payment at the bank or post office with a 'bolletino' attached.*
- *Alternatively, you can arrange for your bank to pay your bills automatically.*
- *Payment via the supplier's Internet site by clicking under the heading 'Controlla e paga'. Most sites accept credit cards such as Visa, Diners, MasterCard and American Express. It is advisable*

*to acquire a 'bancomat' card from your local
bank as certain automatic teller cards can be
used to make utility payments.*

- *Warning: As with automatic payments anywhere
in the world, mistakes can happen. Make sure
you check all bills and credit card charges.*

NOTE ABOUT UTILITY BILLS: Italian utility companies do
not make regular visits to monitor consumption, instead
they estimate annual usage based on your consumption
history. Your bills will reflect this estimation as indicated
by the words '*consumo stimato*'. Your actual usage vs.
the estimate will be adjusted at the end of the year.
This final adjustment notice (which can arrive up to
two months after you vacate a premise) can be quite
a shocker if your usage varies greatly compared to
their estimate.

Possible Monthly Extras:

Portiere (Door Man) Service: If your building shares a
portiere or custodian you're likely to be charged a monthly
fee in addition to your rent. It is customary to acknowledge their services with a small cash 'gift' during the
Christmas holiday season.

Parking: You may have to pay extra for parking your car
or scooter. Garage parking, if not included in the rent,
can cost up to 300+ euro per month (depending on the
size of your vehicle). Cars cannot remain on central streets
unless you have a valid parking pass. (See Chapter Six:
Getting Around). If a garage is included in your rental
fees and you are not using it, ask your landlord for permission to sublet, as there is great demand for parking
in the city center.

Cleaning, Garbage and Laundry

Laundry and Laundromats

If you do not have laundry facilities where you live or they are too small to accommodate large loads, you can go to a local laundry, *lavanderia* or to one of Florence's many public Laundromats *(Lavarapido)*. While clothes-lines work great in the warmer months, clothes often stay damp and stiff for a long time in winter. To remove the last strain of dampness, it's best to take them for a quick spin in a commercial dryer. There are several coin operated Laundromats called 'Wash and Dry', with the name written in blue and green. Some even have internet services on site. They are usually open between 8am and 10 pm. Make sure you bring your own detergent, small bills and lots of change. Water in Florence tends to be 'hard', so it's advisable to always use fabric softener, *ammorbidente*. *Coccolino* is one of the most common brands.

Dry Cleaners *(lavaggio a secco/ tintoria)* There are numerous dry cleaners in Florence. Look around your neighborhood and choose the one closest to you. Note that some require payment ahead of service.

Maid Services

Most landlords or agencies can provide you with of names of people who can offer domestic help. Fees range from 9 to 15 euro per hour and most staff prefer to receive cash. Try asking around, *passa parola*, as recommendations always work best.

Garbage

In Florence, garbage is managed by **QUADRIFOGLIO** (tel. 800/330011). If you live in the city, there are large blue dumpsters on various street corners where you can dispose of your weekly garbage. Some of the bin stations provide options for recycling glass products. If you live in one of the few areas without dumpsters, you may leave your garbage outside the front door of your building after 7:30 am. If you are unsure of garbage collection day either call 800/684001 or watch your neighbors. You'll soon get the rhythm.

Oversize Garbage: You can call 055/7339328 to arrange for a pick up. You will be charged extra for this service.

Understanding Street Numbers

Addresses in Florence can be a bit confusing. It is common to find two of the same number written—one in red and the other in blue or black. Residential addresses in Florence are denoted in large blue lettering while business addresses use smaller red numbers (or at least were a resident or business when the number was assigned....100 years ago). When you read 'via dei Macci 13r' the 'r' refers to *rosso*, and indicates a business. It is interesting to note that the numbers of the streets running parallel to the Arno go from low to high in correspondence with the flow of the river. For streets that run perpendicular to the river, lower numbers are closest to the Arno.

Understanding the Shutter Systems (Heat out or Heat in)

A common feature of Italian buildings is the elaborate shutter systems that frame the windows and doors of homes, shops and restaurants. Artistically speaking, Italy is famous for its nuances of light and hence one can't help wonder why one would want to block it out. After one sweltering summer with the shutters wide open to the view you'll understandwhy they shut them! Shutters are an effective and economical way to screen out day-time heat, keeping interiors cool and alternately in the winter they minimize heat loss.

Summer Use: Keep your shutters closed all day to screen out the hot rays of the sun. As the evening begins to cool, open your shutters to let in cool night breezes.

Winter Use: Keep your shutters closed all night. If there is sun during the day, open them to let in whatever rays might be penetrating the gray skies.

ITALIAN TERMS FOR CHAPTER TWO

Questura :	police headquarters
Comune :	municipality
Circoscrizione :	a subdivision in a municipality
Anagrafe :	the bureau of vital statistics or census office
Ispettorato provinciale del lavoro :	provincial labor office
Libretto di lavoro :	work card

Permesso di soggiorno :	permission to stay in Italy over 90 days
Permesso di lavoro :	work permit
Codice fiscale :	personal tax number
Partita iva :	vat tax number
Marca da bollo :	tax stamp
Carta bollata :	paper with a tax stamp on it
Subentro:	taking over a previous tenant's account
Voltura :	transfering an account
Pagare in nero:	to pay in 'black' – to pay under the table
Pagare in contanti:	to pay in cash
Servizio clienti :	customer service
Numero verde :	toll free number
Conto :	account
Fattura :	invoice
Bolletta :	bill
Data di scadenza :	due date or expiration date
Pagare la bolletta :	to pay the bill
Sportello :	ticket counter/window
Lavarapido :	wash & dry Laundromat
Lavaggio a secco :	dry cleaning
Passa parola :	to ask around, to spread the word

INTERNET TERMS IN ITALIAN
Chiocciola: @
Barra: /
Spazio: space
Trattino basso: underscore

"Italy is a dream that keeps returning for the rest of your life." — Anna Akhmatova

2 SCHOOLS AND KIDS

International Schools

Florence currently has only one accredited school taught entirely in English. The International School of Florence, once known as the American International School of Florence, offers North American based curriculum from Kindergarten to 12th grade. It has two campuses: its Junior

School (K – 5) is located in Bagno a Ripoli—about a 15-minute drive from the center of Florence. The Middle and Upper (High) School is situated in a villa near Piazzale Michelangelo, approximately five minutes from the center by car. ISF offers a high school diploma as well as the International Baccalaureate (IB).

To contact the school or to find out more about admission, fees and curriculum, check out their website at www.isfitaly.org

Addresses:
Junior School (K – 5)
The International School of Florence
Villa le Tavernule, Via del Carota 23/25
50012 Bagno a Ripoli (FI) Italy
Phone: +39 055/644226
admin.tav@isfitaly.org

Middle and Upper School (6 – 12)
The International Schoool of Florence
Villa Torri di Gattaia, Viuzzo di Gattaia, 9
50125 Florence, Italy
Phone: + 39 055 2001515
Fax: + 39 055/ 200 8400
admin.gat@isfitaly.org

Pre and Elementary International Schools

The Canadian Island School
This small private pre-school operates in English and is primarily attended by Italian families who want their children to have early English language experiences.
Via Gioberti 15 – 50121 Florence
Phone: +39 055/677567
www.canadianisland.com

The Westminster International School
An elementary English language school located in Pisa, Westminster also provides special educational initiatives for older children. For more information about their programs and curriculum, check their website.
Via di Goletta 1, Pisa, Italy 56121
Phone: +39 050/2200754
info@westminsterinternationalschool.org
www.westminsterinternationalschool.org

Other Foreign Schools

The French School
Ecole Française de Florence, Victor Hugo
Via Gioberti 67, 50121
Tel: 055/677110
ecole.florence@tiscali.it

Steiner Waldorf School of Florence
Via della Chiesa 4
50020 La Romola, S. Casciano
Tel: 050/2200754

This school's primary language of instruction is German. Its methodology follows the techniques outlined in Steiner Waldorf's curriculum.

Overview of Italian Schools and Curriculum

In Italy all children must attend at least 10 years of compulsory school, usually between the ages of six to sixteen. Regulated by the Ministry of Education, both public and private schools are highly centralized. Elementary schools are somewhat of an exception—most tend to be funded and organized by the municipality. Virtually all schools are slotted into the State system as far as teaching and examinations are concerned.

The school year runs from September to June with minimal holidays at Christmas and Easter. Italian children as young as three years old may start attending a preschool *asilo nido or scuola materna*. These schools are private and not mandatory. Compulsory schooling starts which the *scuola elementare* which children begin attending around age six and runs until they are approximately 11 years of age.

Scuola Media is the next level of schooling for children aged 11 to 14. Middle school is divided into three levels *prima, seconda* and *terza media*. Each progressive year becomes more difficult in terms of academic preparation and focus. Generally students only take oral examinations during their first two years with written exams starting around the *terza* level . At the end of the terza level students take both written and orla exams for all material studied over the three year period. If they pass, they receive their *diploma di licenza media*.

Students are expected to purchase all their books and supplies. Generally subjects are similar to those in North American schools, but most course titles tend to be more specific. For example, Social Studies is divided into 'Anthropology' and 'History'. Art class covers architecture, design, drawing, and painting with teachers favoring a more technical approach. The Italian curriculum is very focused on academics, placing less emphasis on athletics and the arts. Said activities are considered more extra curricular and tend to be organized privately by individual families.

Although Italian law madates schooling until age sixteen many Italian children opt out of the formal system after the scuola media to take on technical trades or follow in family operations. Students who aspire to continue their studies and attend university often enroll in a *liceo* which is something akin to a North American high school. At this stage, courses become more specialized and follow one of three venues of study: *classico* (languages), *artistico* (the arts) or *scientifico* (maths and sciences). Enrollment in a *liceo* generally implies five more years of schooling. Upon receiving their *maturità* diploma, students can enroll in University. Those who graduate from technical institutions may also enter university to complete their studies in related fields.

When considering the financial pros and cons of schooling, Florence's most expensive option is the private English-speaking International School which is approximately three times as expensive as its Italian counterparts. There are several private Italian schools located in or near Florence's city center. These schools have accepted numerous foreign students in the past and are accustomed to assisting foreigners looking for an alternative to the English-speaking International School. Most private Italian schools are Roman Catholic institutions run by the Jesuits. A child doesn't need to be of this denomination to attend. While private Jewish and Protestant schools can be found throughout Italy, Florence only offers primary education in Italian for these two religious denominations.

Enrolling your children in the Italian school system is yet another option. Due to an already over-burdened system, some schools may not be as welcoming to foreigners as their private counterparts. Of course, any EU citizen may apply for attendance at a state run school. The curriculum follows the Italian system and all instruction is in Italian. Public schools are free, although non EU nationals should expect a minimum fee of approximately 400 euro.

Private Italian Schools In Florence

Istituto Sacro Cuore
viale Michaelangelo, 27
Phone: 055/6811872 Fax: 055/6811388
www.sacrocuore.com.

Istituto Statale SS Annunziata
Piazzale del Poggio Imperiale
Tel: 055/226171 Fax: 055/2298085
www.poggio-imperiale.it

Public Schools in Florence:
Check with the municipality to find the one nearest your residence.

UNIVERSITIES AND STUDY ABROAD PROGRAMS

For a complete list visit the English version of: wwwintoscana.it under 'Schools and Courses'.

Extra Curricular Activities for Kids

Your kid's after-school needs will depend on the age of your children and the school they're attending. Since Italian schools focus primarily on academics, after-school hours are used to flesh out student activities in fields like music, dance and athletics. Throughout Florence there are numerous private extra-curricular schools offering lessons in dance, music, theater and art designed to spark a child's interest and participation. One noteworthy school is the celebrated Fiesole School of Music, which provides advanced programming in choral music, instrument instruction and operatic studies. Most students must audition in order to attend. Instruction is in both Italian and English.

For a listing of schools, teachers and private lessons in a variety of disciplines, from sports to the arts, check The Essential White Pages at the back.

Swimming Pools

Florence's largest and most popular public swimming complex is the **COSTOLI** (tel: 055/6236027). Located near the Stadium at Campo di Marte, it hosts three pools. A frequently used city managed facility is the **Piscina Nannini Bellarvia** (tel: 055/677521). This swimming center occasionally offers the bonus of evening openings. The **Piscina Le Pavoniere** in the Cascine Park. (tel: 055/362233) is also quite nice, but the pool has an L shape so it's not a length swimmer's ideal. Entrance costs vary from 4 to 6 euro per person and the pools are open from 8am to 11pm though it's best to play it safe and call ahead to confirm. Of course, there are many other pools around Florence. Some are associated with clubs or private gyms and require the purchase of a season ticket.

Tennis, Running Tracks, Gyms and Private Clubs

There are several tennis clubs in and around Florence as well as various running tracks. The Assi facility is located right across from the International School's middle/upper campus on viale Michelangelo. Its tennis courts and track are both available for use at a nominal fee. In addition, you can find clubs like Virgin Active that offer a full range of sports complexes as well as fitness gyms and classes. Please refer to The Essential White Pages at the back for specific names, locations and phone numbers. Some of these clubs require membership and others accept drop-ins. Most instruction is in Italian although some coaches and instructors do speak English.

Horse Riding

English horse-back riding is a favorite sport in Tuscany and there are several arenas and schools in the nearby hills as well as right in Florence's Cascine park. These schools provide both private and group lessons and some supply the horse and any necessary equipment. Lessons are in Italian. There is one Western School near Ugolino (about a 15 minute drive south of Florence). Their early morning Saturday classes are particularly splendid in the spring and summer when the sky still has its reddish glow and the temperatures still cool. (See The Essential White Pages).

Golf

Located 25 km from Florence along the road to Chianti, you'll find the Ugolino Golf Club. This golf course takes full advantage its natural surroundings. The first nine holes are very challenging due to the hilly terrain. While the remaining nine are on more even ground, they are nonetheless demanding. Players have to face small, well-defended green areas and differences in levels and hazards.

Facilities: Driving range; 12 open on the grass, 8 covered, putting green, tennis courts, swimming pool, pro shop, snack bar and restaurant. Open year-round. Closed Mondays. Visitor times: Tuesdays-Fridays, except 11:30am to 2:30pm

Circolo del Golf dell'Ugolino
via Chiantigiana 3 - 50015 Grassina - Firenze
Tel. 055/2301009 - Fax 055/2301141
info@golfugolino.it

Other golf courses:
Golf Club Casentino, Via Fronzola 6, (Palazzo Poppi), Arezzo
Poggio Dei Medici Via S. Gavino, 27 Cignano
Tel: 055 8430436
www.poggiodeimedici.it

Castelfalfi Country Club in Montaione
Tel: 0571 6983
www.castelfalfi.it

Baseball

Baseball junkies will be happy to hear that Florence has its own Italian baseball/softball association called Federazione Italiana Baseball e Softball. For more information visit www.fibstoscana.it or tel: 055/4625100.

Things for Kids:

Florence is more than just a city packed with fine art and architecture. Florentines enjoy outdoor sports, amusement centers, golf and cinema as well. Due to the tight quarters of the historic center, most of these types of activities are located in the periphery outside the city walls. There you can find large cinemaplex style theatres, bowling alleys, theme parks, zoos and even baseball and soccer associations. The Essential White Pages at the back lists some of the larger and more popular leisure options. Spread the word, *passa parola*, that you are looking for a specific type of activity either for yourself or your children—the Florentines will be able to direct you best. Most facilities are Italian-speaking and require a car, bus or bike for access.

A valuable listing of special events and activities for children and families can be found in the 'Kid's Activities' section of **The Florentine**. Published bi-weekly, this newspaper is an excellent source for discovering seasonal events happening in or near Florence.

Day Adventures
MondoBimbo Inflatables
Parterre, Piazza della Liberta, San Lorenzo This is a great place for your under 10's to let off some steam while

jumping on oversized inflatable snakes, dogs, castles, etc. Make sure to bring extra socks and be aware that they do not accept credit cards.
Tel: 055/5532946

Canadian Island Pre-School and Daycare
A great place to drop youngsters for fun, creative activities conducted entirely in English.
Tel: 055/677567 or visit www.canadianisland.com

Out of Town:
Giardino Zoologico, Pistoia
Just 30 minutes from Florence, you'll find this game park where you can take your kids to see the giraffes, rhinos, lemurs and crocodiles. Check for seasonal hours and openings.
Tel: 057/83911219 or visit www.zoodipistoia.it

Parco Giochi Cavallino Matto
The largest fun fair of the coastal region, this park is located in Livorno so check ahead for operation hours and seasonal openings.
Phone: 0565/745720 or visit www.cavallinomatto.it

Parco Pinocchio
Located in Collodi, about an hour drive west of Florence, this small outdoor park tells the famous story of Pinocchio using interactive sculptures.
Phone: 0572/429342 or visit www.pinocchio.it

ENGLISH CINEMA:
For English language cinema, visit the **Odeon Theatre**, located in the center of Florence at Piazza Strozzi 2. The theatre shows a variety of current Hollywood releases usually on Monday, Tuesday and Thursday nights. Check their website for times and shows: *www.cinehall.it* Tel. 055/214068.

The **British Institute** at Lungarno Guicciardini 9 has a weekly program of classic English-speaking cinema, usually on Wednesday nights.
Tel: 055/267781 - 055/26778200 or visit www.britishinstitute.it

Parks

Florence is not a very 'green' city and finding clean public parks for playing catch or going for a 'swing' is a bit of a challenge. On the gates of small community parks throughout Florence you will find notices regarding hours and usage. In the historic center, try visiting the **Piazza D'Azeglio Park**. It has some amusement equipment for smaller children but does not offer much in the way of grass or greenery. Near the neighborhood of San Niccolò, just across the Arno try **Parco Carraia,** a small park that's great for kids who want to throw a ball around or just get out for a stretch and play. It's a lovely stroll up from Porta San Minato just below Piazzale Michelangelo.

Le Cascine is Florence's largest public park. It offers playgrounds, trails along the Arno and hosts several sporting complexes (pools, tennis courts, horseback riding and race tracks). On weekends, you'll find the area a-buzz with picnickers and vendors. Its entrance is near Ponte della Vittoria outside the Western City Gates.

The Boboli Gardens are situated just south of the Ponte Vecchio in the Oltarno district behind Palazzo Pitti. Considered one of Italy's most important gardens, it's a renowned open-air museum that displays ancient and modern statues, fountains, walkways, vistas and greenery. Developed over the centuries, this garden is open daily from 8:30am to 5:30pm. You must arrive at least one hour prior to closing to be allowed entrance. Daily entrance fees apply, though annual memberships are also available. If you join the Amici degli Uffizi (see *Chapter: Four* for details) entrance is free. Tel: 055/2651816.

Unfortunately, many of the wonderful gardens in Florence are privately owned and hidden behind high walls. It's possible to view some of these by appointment—though most are not child-friendly. *Gardens of Florence and Tuscany* by Mariachiara Pozzana is a great resource book with contact information and instructions on how to set up visits. Published by Giunti, this small book is a treasure-chest of daily adventures for anyone seeking green vistas. In addition, there are several agencies that organize weekly garden tours of Fiesole and Tuscany.

Babysitting Services

There are several groups that can assist with babysitting services. The local American Church often has a list of young ladies who can provide short term sitting. They also have a Church nursery. Contact them at www.stjamesnursery.com

Agency Eruo-pair provides sitters and au paris. Locatd on Viag Ghibelline 96R Tel: 055 242181.

Agenzia Help provides various services on Via Bolognese 4A R, Tel: 055 470333.

Teenagers and Cultural Challenges

Liquor: One of the biggest challenges for visitors with teenagers is that liquor and late nightclubs are easily accessible to young people in Italy. The legal drinking age in Italy is 16 though no one really tends to monitor it. During family dinners, Italian children are often offered samples of the same wine and after meal *digestivi* as the adults. Generations of Italians have grown up with wine and spirits as a prevalent part of their culture. Generally speaking, they view alcohol less as a means of intoxication and more as a staple in the enjoyment of life. Share this message with your kids and be aware of potential situations in which your teenagers may find themselves. Ultimately, we must take responsibility for teaching our kids the importance of drinking responsibly. Drunken foreigners are not a pretty sight and leave a damaging reputation for all parties.

Drugs: In this regard, Italy is similar to North America: drugs are available, they are accessible and they are, of course, illegal. If you are caught taking, selling or carrying illegal drugs you will be taken before a magistrate. Depending on your intentions, you may be able to leave the country with nothing more than a fine. However, if the authorities discover or suspect that you are in possession of, or dealing illegal drugs, you can end up with a prison sentence of up to 20 years. If you find yourself or your children in a position where you require assistance, contact your nearest consulate or embassy. They will refer you to appropriate legal counsel.

Late Nights: Comparatively, Italian children tend to stay up later than North Americans. Evening meals are often not served until 8:30-9:00pm so it is no surprise that youth stay out late. On weekends, older kids are out well after what would be deemed a reasonable curfew in North America. Parties, nightclubs and popular evening clubs tend to be located outside the city center which implies extra travel time via taxis or cars. It is common for kids to sleep in the country on weekends rather than returning to the city center—a cultural habit that often causes a fair amount of anxiety amongst foreign parents. Use your common sense about regulating whom your children are with, what they are doing and how they are traveling.

"All time spent out of Italy is time misspent" — *Mathew Arnold*

4 WORK, STUDY AND SOCIAL

Working in Florence

Legalities about working

In order to work legally in Italy you are required to have a working visa unless you have a valid EEC passport. A working visa needs to be processed in your country of origin and can be obtained from your local Italian

Consulate once your employer has provided proof of employment. Students who have a 'permesso di soggiorno' are allowed to work up to 20 hours a week legally.

Major Employers of Foreigners in Florence

In terms of its size, Florence is not a major city in Italy, thus, doesn't have the same international commercial and consular representation as Milan or Rome. There are only two English-speaking countries represented with consular offices: the United States and Great Britain. Major foreign employers in Florence are General Electric and the pharmaceutical company Eli Lilly. Numerous study abroad programs with adjunct campuses to American and British Universities and the International School of Florence employ professors and staff from outside of Italy.

Work Agencies in Florence that provide job searches for foreigners with legal work permits:

Adecco Temp Agency
Via Baracca 2
Tel: 055/368548
www. adecco.it

Manpower
Via Cavour 231
Tel: 055/282921
www.manpower.it

Info Lavoro
Via Cavour 37
Tel: 055/4269542
www.provincia.firenze.it/infolavoro

SOCIAL

Living in a foreign country can be exciting and sometimes lonely. Language is often the first barrier. As an Anglophone, you are not alone in Florence. There is a relatively large English-speaking community throughout Tuscany providing social groups, classes, circulations and special events. To search out these groups stop by English-speaking consulates, schools, bookstores and churches. All of these venues are good places to find support and discover ways to get involved in the community. Florence is rich in traditions related to food, wine, art and architecture. Many Anglophone social groups participate in activities that help members learn and appreciate some of the differences between cultures.

Learning the Language

Italians are a warm and hospitable people with a long history of hosting foreigners. Many Italians speak English well and an Anglophone can easily travel and live in some parts of Italy with only a smattering of the Italian language at their disposal. Nonetheless, it is worth the effort to learn at least a bit of Italian, if only as a courtesy to your hosts. More importantly, it will open new opportunities for you to experience this culture and its people on a more intimate level.

Learning a new language can be difficult and frustrating so avoid setting impossible goals for yourself. There are a myriad of language schools in Florence; some offer cultural studies or cooking lessons while others focus strictly on the language and grammar. When searching out the course that's right for you, think about your reasons for learning the language and your everyday needs.

Do you need it for conversation or do you wish to write and work in Italian as well? These considerations will help you determine the type of course you ultimately choose.

FOOD, WINE AND ART CLASSES

Throughout the city, you'll find an abundance of schools and institutions—both private and public—that offer courses related to the study and consumption of Italian cultural products. Venture into English-speaking book-stores like *McRae's Books, Paperback Exchange or Edison* where you'll find brochures providing ideas for numerous opportunities. Whether you are looking for serious, for-mal courses or a more casual environment for learning about Italian food markets and cooking or shopping for ingredients—there is something for everyone. The tourist information center on via Cavour next to the Palazzo Medici also has a listing of agencies and schools offer-ing one-of-a-kind day trips or longer courses. Check out local travel agencies in the center—many can provide names of nearby villas for day trips. Some options include tours through private cellars, culinary adventures or art and architecture walking tours.

The Amici degli Uffizi Pass

Whether you're living in Florence or just visiting the city for a couple of days, it's worth purchasing an annual membership card to the Uffizi Gallery. The 'Amici degli Uffizi' – (Friends of the Uffizi) is a pass that provides its owners with wonderful benefits. With your membership, you get 'front of the line' privileges and free access to many state museums including the Academia and the Uffizi—which alone are worth the membership. You are also granted exclusive visits to the galleries and receive special invitations to exhibitions and cultural events as well as a subscription to the club's newspaper. It really is the best deal in town!

At time of pringting membership costs 60 euro per person. A family of four with children under 18 pay 100 euro. If you are under 26 years old, annual membership is 25 euro. To apply for your membership online visit www. amicidegliuffizi.com or you can pick up a pass at the Uffizi gallery offices on the west side of the courtyard across from the main entrance. Note: you need a picture ID—usually a passport, which serves to identify you as the exclusive pass holder.

Membership grants you free entrance to the following museums:

Uffizi Gallery
Pitti Palace
Giardino dei Boboli
San Marco Museum
Accademia Gallery
Bargello Museum
The Medici Chapels
Cenacolo by Andrea del Sarto
Medici Villa - La Petraia
Medici Villa at Poggio a Caiano

A coffee by any other name
   By Suzi Jenkins

You would never have believed anything so simple as having a cup of coffee could possibly be so complicated; but once you really understand Italian coffee you'll appreciate and indeed hold in great esteem the greatest of all Italian rituals – 'prendere un caffè' (having a coffee).

What?

Espresso: the short, hot blast of dense, dark coffee that is to be drunk straight away without letting it cool down.Unless you specify otherwise you will get the standard measure, however, the espresso can also come in two other versions; 1) basso, corto or ristretto (three ways of saying, 'even smaller'), or 2) alto or lungo (slightly larger). Real connoisseurs sometimes claim that the only way to really taste the coffee is to drink it from a glass and not from a china cup – hence on top of many espresso machines you will see four or five small shot glasses. Want to try it? - caffè in vetro are the magic words. Many Italians do take their espresso with sugar, or artificial sweetener (dolcificante). One important note – in Tuscany the words caffè and espresso are interchangeable; order a caffè and you will be served an espresso!

Espresso Macchiato: the same espresso, but with a dash of either hot (macchiato caldo) or cold (macchiato freddo) or frothy (macchiato con la schiuma) milk. This variety of coffee is generally taken without sugar.

Caffè Americano: this variety is absolutely nothing like an American coffee! It is an espresso, served in a large cup that has been topped up with a dash of hot water to dilute the coffee just a little.

Caffè Corretto: literally a coffee that has been 'corrected' – normally with a generous dash of spirits (rum, brandy, whisky). Adds an extra kick!

Espresso doppio: not for the faint-hearted. A double whack of caffeine in a double espresso! Don't venture this one or you are liable to be up all night pacing the floor or bouncing off ceilings.

Caffè freddo: a rather recent invention for the hot summer months – an espresso coffee shaken up with ice and sugar, served in a glass. A good bar will make one for you there and then, although nowadays many bars do have pre-prepared bottles at the ready, and you can even find it in cans in the supermarket!

Cappuccino: an espresso served in a larger cup that is topped to the brim with hot frothy milk. You can ask for a cappuccino bollente (boiling hot) or tiepido (lukewarm). You can even ask for the addition of cacao in polvere (a dusting of bitter coco powder). A cappuccino senza schiuma is a cappuccino without froth. Feel free to add sugar or not, as you prefer.

Caffè Latte: now we start getting complicated! This is essentially the same as a cappuccino without froth, but may well be served in a tall glass rather than a cup. Generally there is a higher milk to coffee ratio than in a cappuccino. People drink caffè latte at home, not in bars.

Latte macchiato: once again, served in a high glass, this is basically a glass of hot milk, with a tiny dash of coffee (the reverse of the caffè latte!). The milk is poured in first, and the coffee is added afterwards.

And an important ingredient that you may wish to use in any of the above is caffè decaffeinato (decaffeinated coffee). Or perhaps you might try an 'orzo', made from caffeine-free ground barley.

Keep in mind that this is just the abbreviated list – any good Italian will be able to come up with another 20 versions that are not included here, but if you get to grips with this lot, then you are well on your way to knowing enough about coffee to avoid any major faux pas, AND ordering something you like too!

When?

Every coffee has a right and wrong time to be taken. Follow the Italian lead – they have been doing it for an awfully long time!

Cappuccino, caffè-latte, latte macchiato: for breakfast, as a mid-morning 'snack', and conceivably as a mid-afternoon 'snack' in winter (Italians on the run might use it to replace a meal). A cappuccino and brioche or pastry is a great way to start the day and very often it leaves room to repeat the experience at mid-morning too, without killing your appetite for lunch!

BUT, NOT EVER AFTER A MEAL!

Of course, Italians eat very well, and quite rightly take great pride in their cuisine. Possibly one of the most offensive ways of ending a meal is by asking for a cappuccino. Here we have referred to it as a snack – indeed it is a large cup of warm milk, and very filling. Ending your meal with a cappuccino (apart from constituting a violent assault on your digestive system!) implies that you have not eaten well or sufficiently. If you cannot manage an espresso then try learning this phrase: 'Un caffè americano con tantissima acqua calda, e un po' di latte freddo a parte.' (An espresso coffee with lots of hot water, and some cold milk on the side)!!! Any Italian waiter worth his salt will call this 'dishwater' once out of your hearing...or perhaps even well within your hearing! But you will get something approaching an Anglo-Saxon watery coffee that you can drink, and that doesn't (drastically) upset the cook!

Article reprinted from The Florentine - Issue 4 - May 12, 2005

Entertainment, Events and Hospitality

What's Happening?
There's always something happening when it comes to theatre, music, art, festivals, markets, cinema, exhibitions and concerts in and around Florence. Surprisingly, these events are not always well-marketed and you really need to be on the watch for great opportunities. To access information regarding weekly/monthly events in Florence scour the EVENTS IN FLORENCE pages of *The Florentine* newspaper. You can also track everything on their website at ***www.theflorentine.net.***

Other Sources:
Firenze Spetacolo is an Italian newspaper that prints a few sections in English. It's a useful guide for news, local events and performances taking place in Florence and throughout Tuscany.

The following websites are also available for your reference:
www.intoscana.it
www.communie.fi.it

Newspapers and Magazines in Florence:
You will find a myriad of newsstands and book stores throughout Florence where you can buy the Italian newspapers *La Nazione, La Repubblica* and other local papers. There are two free daily newspapers in Florence called *Leggo and City* (both are printed in Italian). Foreign newspapers and magazines are available at newsstands in the train station and in the larger bookstores in central Florence. *The Herald Tribune* and *USA Today* are printed and distributed daily in Italy.

Buying Tickets to Events

For tickets to most events you can phone the organizer directly and pay on site when you arrive (usually cash only).

Another place to gather information and purchase tickets is the Florence Box Office: ***www.boxoffice.it.*** They except credit cards and have a branch on via Alamanni 39 (behind SMN train station). Tel. 055/210804.

For larger events, you can e-book with a credit card on ***www.intoscana.it/shop.***

Concerts, dances and live performances usually take place at the following venues:

Teatro Verdi
Via Ghibellina 99
Tel. 055/212320
www.teatroverdifirenze.it
Note: Pre-show purchases are sometimes available at the Teatro Verdi box office on via Ghibellina 99. Tel: 055/212320. They do not accept credit cards so plan to pay in cash or by bancomat.

Mandela Forum Palasport
Viale Paoli
Tel: 055/667566
www.mandelaforum.it

Teatro Communale (Maggio Musicale)
Via Solferino 15
Tel. 055/27791
www. maggiomusicalefiorentino.it

The Saschall
Lungarno Aldo Moro 3
Tel. 055/6503068

Artemio Franchi
This is the football arena and a great place to attend outdoor summer concerts.
Viale Fanti 4/6
Tel. 055/210804

Tenax
Via Pratese 46
Tel: 055/308160

Hospitality

Initially you may find it easier to meet and socialize with ex-pats than with Italians. Although friendly, Florentines tend to be reserved socially, so you may need to extend the first invite. A typical way to break the ice is to go for an 'aperitivo' at one of the numerous bars or *enoteche* in Florence. The proper time for a drink is around 6pm to 7:30pm, before heading home after work. If you extend the invite it's polite for you to pick up the bill.

It is the social norm for Italians to entertain and socialize in restaurants more than in their homes. If you are invited to someone's house, it's customary to bring a small hostess gift of some sort, such as pastries or flowers. Typically, you can expect a selection of munchies at the beginning of the evening accompanied by drinks. If the nibbles are casual chips and nuts, the meal following will be informal. However, if you are greeted with an array of hors d'oeuvres, crostini and a selection of prosecco, you're probably in for a gastronomic feast with two or three courses and digestivi afterwards. When you take leave, thank the host and hostess. It's customary to make a follow-up thank you call the next day or even to send flowers depending on the type of event.

OBSERVATIONS ON EATING IN ITALY

Meals: Breakfast, usually a croissant and cappuccino, is eaten standing up. In Italy, the only place to find eggs or cereal are in hotels for tourists. The working man goes to the same trattoria for lunch every day, and this ritual replaces the tradition of going home and eating with the family. In Italy, there is no such thing as eating at your desk, in your car or on the bus. Even on trains, Italians go to the dining car, and avoid eating at their seats. Meals are a time for eating and relaxing, not for meeting or discussing business.

Snacking: Generally speaking, people do not 'snack' in Italy. Children have an afternoon snack, 'merenda', but it's a privilege reserved for children only. Italians never eat while reading, driving, walking or talking on the phone. Although there are malls in Italy, you don't find locals walking around shopping centers with food or cups.

Seasonal foods: Italians don't pick out a recipe and then go buy the ingredients. They go to the market, look at what is in season and then decide what to cook. The same is true in restaurants where menus change by the season. The ingredients are always fresh, ripe and the flavor of Italian food does not come from sauces but from the use of quality ingredients.

Refrigerators: An Italian refrigerator is usually empty! Many people buy their food one day at a time. They go to the market daily, and the portions they choose are 'just right'. Leftovers are a strange phenomenon, and doggy bags are for tourists (and dogs) only.

Shopping: Don't be surprised if the vendor asks you when you plan to eat the fruit you purchase. It helps him evaluate the level of ripeness you need. (Your choices are either 'today' or 'tomorrow'— if you planned on eating the melon three days from now, why would you be buying it today?)

Before the butcher will give you the cut of meat you've chosen, he'll demand to know how you are going to cook it. It's almost like going to an animal shelter, they're not going to let you take it home unless they know you'll be treating it right.

Wine shops: Not only do you have to tell the shop owner what kind of food you will be serving with the wine, you have to describe how it will be cooked. Different wines are served according to whether your lamb is sautéed, broiled or baked.

Slow food: An organization called 'Slow Food' started in Italy several years ago when the first McDonald's was opened. They sponsor cooking classes, oil tastings, conferences. Restaurants identify themselves as a 'slow food' member by placing the logo (a snail) on the door, which certifies that the restaurant is committed to upholding traditional processes while cooking with top quality, 'thoughtful' ingredients.

Eating Out in Florence

Compared to Anglo cultures dining hours are slightly later in Italy. Lunch is served around 1– 2:30pm and kitchens close after 2:30pm with little available until until dinner. If you miss the lunch hour you can always grab a sandwich, *panino,* at the bars. Dinner starts around 8:30 – 9:00 pm. Many eating establishments take *prenotazioni* or reservations. In winter, they are not essential, but in spring, summer and early fall it's wise to call ahead. Most restaurants are closed Sunday evenings and all day Monday. Those located in the historic center tend to keep longer hours in the prime tourist months.

Restaurant or Trattoria?

You will notice a diverse range of eating establishments in Florence. In the past each had a distinct status, but their characteristics have become more blurred over the years. For example, in today's city a traditionally cheaper *trattoria* can be as expensive as a *ristorante*.

Listed below is a generalized overview of the different ways to eat out in Florence.

Ristorante – usually implies a semi luxurious eating establishment with linens, stemware and a formal dining experience with a higher price point.

Osteria – refers to a casual place to go for drinks and a light meal—something like today's' *enoteca*. It's also similar to a trattoria, though it tends to be more expensive.

Trattoria – is the most common type of eating establishment in Italy today. It suggests a home-style meal with checkered tablecloths, casual service and house wines. Once the place for an inexpensive home-cooked meal, many owners have adopted the popular 'trattoria' brand image but upped the prices due to tourist demand.

Pizzeria – as the name suggests, this is the place to find pizzas. Some trattorias will also serve pizzas. This is considered the simplest and cheapest type of dining experience. Note that Italians may drink beer with pizza, not wine.

Enoteca – this term has everything to do with wine. It can denote a wine store , a wine bar or a restaurant that prides itself on its excellent wine list. Numerous wine bars around Florence are becoming increasingly popular. They open after 4pm for an *aperitivo*, a glass of wine and some nibbles. Many *enoteche*, wine bars will serve free munchies alongside a glass of wine or other alcoholic beverage.

Tavola Calda - implies a cafeteria style establishment that offers hot pre-prepared food that you can select from the bar, rather than the menu. Meals are generally fast, high quality and cheap. (This term is also used to denote the 'meal of the day' which has a special price.)

Fiaschetteria - not as popular as they once were, fiaschetterie are a place to get a drink and a light meal. They are often a rustic addition to a trattoria-style restaurant.

Bars:
The word 'bar' in Italy does not have the same connotation as it does in North America. An Italian bar is the local corner café, where people grab their coffee, pastries, lunch or in between meal *panino* and snack. Bars in Italy do offer alcoholic beverages but there is no age limit for entry. You can either sit at a table and order

from a waiter or you go directly to the cashier and pay for your order. Once you receive your *scontrino*, receipt, you then approach the *barista,* server, behind the counter and announce your order. Beverages, sandwiches and pastries are most often eaten while standing at the counter. At some bars you can buy cigarettes, phone cards and even bus passes.

Menu Reading

Italians like to eat more than one course per meal and they usually order everything 'a la carte' style. Seldom do all your food groups make it onto one plate—each dish is ordered separately and often shared amongst the table.

Antipasti – starters are meant to whet the appetite and usually include a selection of sliced meats, cheeses, olives and grilled vegetables.

Primi – first courses in Italy include soup, pasta, rice or even lightly filled crepès.

Secondi – second courses can be meat or fish—generally grilled, baked or sautèed. Florentines love their traditional cut of beef, and meats feature prominently on menus over fish, which is more common in the coastal towns and cities. *Secondi* are served simply and on their own. Do not expect to see accompaniments unless you order them from the *contorni* section of the menu.

Contorni – are the side dishes that flesh out the second course. Usually roast or fried potatoes, grilled vegetables, spinach, asparagus or whatever vegetable is fresh and in season.

Insalate – Salads are usually eaten after the main meal as they help digest.

Dolci – desserts
Coffee and teas are served after dessert not with it.

Formaggi – cheeses

Digestivi – digestive drinks and dessert wines are often complimentary after a meal.

RESTAURANT TERMINOLOGY

panino :	sandwich
prenotazione :	reservation
ristorante :	restaurant - usually the highest caliber for an eating establishment
trattoria :	home style meal restaurant
osteria :	casual place more to go for drinks
pizzeria :	pizza parlor
enoteca :	wine store/bar
antipasti :	starters
primi :	first courses
contorni :	side dishes
dolci :	desserts
formaggi :	cheeses
digestivi :	dessert wines

The oldest fast food in Florence
By Deirdre Pirro

Any time from about 11:30 in the morning until into the evening, small crowds of people can be seen standing around mobile kiosks on street corners or in squares dotted about the centre of Florence. With their boiling cauldrons, marble or glass counters and stools on the pavement, these kiosks attract students, bankers, housewives, bricklayers, pensioners and, more and more often, discerning tourists - all with one common desire. They are all impatiently awaiting for the **trippaio** (tripe seller) to hand them over a plate of fast food Florentine-style: a dish of tripe or steaming hot **lampredotto** roll.

A sight very seldom seen in other Italian cities, the trippaio has been selling his delicious snacks on Florentine streets for well over one hundred years and is an institution in the city. Today, some of the best known trippai include the **trippaio del Porcellino** found at the back of Piazza del Mercato Nuovo (commonly known as the Straw Market), **Marione**, situated inside the San Lorenzo Market and, my favourite, the father and son tripe dynasty, Sergio and Pierpaolo, who are strategically placed and unashamedly do a roaring trade outside one of Florence's most fashionable restaurants near the market of Sant' Ambrogio.

Sergio explained to me how he came into the game. 'I worked', he said, 'in the retail clothing trade until a little over ten years ago when the pitch in via dei Macci became available. Of course, you can't just set up anywhere you like but you have to wait until another trippaio retires or wants to give up his licence. As the idea of belonging to one of the 'elite' of the five or six trippai working within the walls of the old city had always appealed to me, I jumped at the chance. In fact, there has always been a stall on my site for over a century and, in the future, my son will be here to carry it on.' He added the only downside he could see to the job was 'when it's freezing cold and pelting with rain' but, then again, he reflected, 'that's when I do some of my best business'.

The trippaio's work involves preparing and cooking **tripe** and **lampredotto**, once considered poor man's fare but now a gastronomic delicacy. Tripe is the inner lining of the first of a cow's four stomachs whereas lampredotto comes from the fourth and last stomach. Traditionally, lampredotto is said to take its name from the **lampreda**, a fish similar to an eel, because when it is cooked, it has the same dark colour and looks like the cooked fish. Although decidedly ugly in appearance, lampredotto is the softest and leanest part of the meat and is found exclusively on tripe kiosks only in Florence.

The basic equipment of the trippaio has changed over time thanks to the advent of the small mini-van instead of the heavy hand or pushcart he used to use for transporting his wares and portable gas or electric hot plates used for cooking instead of a glowing brazier. The end product has, nevertheless, remained the same. The trippaio spoons out a bowl of tripe or fishes a piece of lampredotto out of the one of the two pots of broth he has had on the boil since early morning, he cuts it into long strips, seasons it with salt and pepper, puts it in a roll which has been dipped in the broth, dresses it with either a little green or hot sauce and hands it to his customer in exchange for about 3 euro. The customer then usually washes this down with a glass of Chianti or a cold beer whilst exchanging opinions on the latest football scores or the upcoming elections with his neighbour sitting on the stool next to him.

In the past, **Larousse Gastro-nomique** tells us that the likes of Homer, William the Conqueror and Napoleon all enjoyed their tripe. However, in some parts of today's overfed industrialised world, cooking offal has fallen from favour and there are even those who express 'horror' at the very idea of eating it. Despite this, tripe has always been a popular dish in Tuscany. Part of its appeal is that it can be prepared in a variety of different ways and it can be found on the menus of many typical restaurants and trattorie, one of the best known being the restaurant **Bella Ciao**, located just outside Florence. The most famous recipes include **trippa alla fiorentina** (tripe Florence-style) which is cooked in a tomato sauce, and the version from Lucca which has a butter and parmesan cheese base.

If, therefore, you have never tasted tripe or savoured a lampredotto roll, I recommend you do so because what you will be trying is nothing short of a true Florentine experience.

Article originally printed in The Florentine Issue 33 – May 18, 2006

Religion:

Italy is primarily a Catholic country and Sunday is a day for relaxation and family time. Most businesses are closed (except for stores located in the center). Car entrance to Florence's historic center is usually unlimited on Sunday and parking is free on the street. Most garages tend to be closed. The city generally stays quiet until late afternoon when many people flock to the streets for a *passeggiata*, evening stroll, before or after dinner.

Catholic churches are numerous in Florence and mass is usually offered around 10am at most churches. Those who attend mass still dress up as a sign of respect. Most churches will not allow entrance to people wearing shorts, mini skirts or tank tops.

Catholic Masses in English:
At the Duomo on Saturday evenings at 5pm.
At SS Annunziata's side chapel (Cappela degli artisti) on Sundays at 10am

Other denominations:

Baptist Church on Borgo Ognissanti 4, Tel: 055/210537
Jewish Communita Israelitica, via L. Farini 4, Tel: 055/245252

Shir Hadash Jewish reform/progressive congregation: 348/6913059 or 348/9362564

Lutheran Evangelist, via del Bardi 20, Tel: 055/2342775

St. Mark's English Church (Anglican), via Maggio 16/18, Tel: 055/293764

Saint James American Church (Episcopalian) via Rucellai Bernardo 13 Tel: 055/294417

"Report of fashions in proud Italy Whose
manners still our tardy-apish
nation Limps after in base imitation"

— William Shakespeare

5 SHOPPING

Shopping rituals are different in Italy compared to North
America. Large central grocery stores, drug retailers and

big box suppliers are not as common in Italy. Open markets, specialty shops and limited shopping hours are the norm.

Groceries and Staples

There are several ways to buy your groceries in Italy. While one respects the tradition of small stores and daily markets, the other takes advantage of the growing popularity of big North American style superstores. If you choose to shop traditionally, note that every neighborhood has its array of specialty stores for daily bread, milk, cheese, sausages and staples, supplemented by the outdoor markets where seasonal fresh produce is trucked in daily from nearby farms. Although this method of shopping is more time consuming, it often guarantees fresher products and less wastage. It's also a wonderful way to practice your Italian and experience the local culture.

Market

Markets play an important social and economical role in the daily life of Italians. At the marketplace, one can still witness the foundations of commercial exchange between individuals and observe the dynamics of relationship. Numerous markets in Florence are open daily and offer a wide variety of produce as well as a mix of household and personal goods. Seasonal markets crop up throughout the year featuring small producers of specialty items. Almost every small town in Italy hosts a weekly market. Great for special finds, out of town market shopping makes for a wonderful day away from the bustle of Florence. For a listing of out of town markets check The *Florentine's* Events Pages under *Markets and Fairs*.

Florence Markets

Florence's largest and best markets are located in San Lorenzo and Sant' Ambrogio. Shopping for food is a daily ritual which should take place in the early morning as the best merchandise gets picked over by knowledgeable local family chefs. Wake up early and make your way to the market, trolley in tow, to begin your selection of daily needs. If you don't own a trolley buy one! They can be found at markets for as little as 10 euro and are worth every cent!

Florentine city dwellers tend to shop for short-term needs as freshness is a top priority and storage is limited. Remember that some vendors do not like customers to handle the produce so always ask permission before you touch. If in doubt about what something is or what you are looking for' just ask the vendors. As a rule, they are generally very happy to give you advice, recipes and suggestions for serving the seasonal selections presented. The best thing about market shopping is that after several visits you begin to develop a *familiarità* with the vendors. This valuable and engaging form of familiar rapport is earned through daily patronage with shop owners, market vendors and even bar servers and it's a top-notch antidote to the chaotic flurry of city life.

There are seven main daily markets in Florence— some of which offer redundant wares and others that are specialized in gastronomic produce. Each is worth a visit.

Price Bartering

There are still many vendors willing to negotiate with buyers to achieve a mutually perceived fair value for the exchange. Some visitors, unfamiliar with this type of 'purchaser power', fear dishonest dealings within the negotiating process. Undoubtedly, the adage of 'buyer beware' holds true everywhere. Nonetheless, when a transaction is respectful and politely negotiated with a bit of humor, it often proves a mutual win.

In markets such as San Lorenzo and Mercato Centrale one should be more cautious when bartering. Swollen with tourists in the summer months, these market stalls are often manned by very aggressive vendors. Many are not Italian and cannot speak more than a smattering of the language. They sell commodities on a mass basis and are well-versed on the tourist optic of negotiating. It's common for some vendors to initially set the prices high and quickly offer the buyer a discount, *sconto*. Beware of these tactics as usually the immediately offered discount price is still relatively high. However, if the merchandise is something you really want to purchase, you can still offer your best price and see where it leads. Some may rebuff you, others will continue the discussion openly and with fervor. If you look carefully and spend some time talking to the vendors, you'll realize that some are selling traditional products in which they take great pride.

Bartering is not acceptable in large chain stores and in smaller shops where you can see signs stating *prezzi fissi* or 'fixed prices'. Some shop owners are willing to discuss a *sconto* based on a large cash purchase or if you are buying several items.

SUPERMARKET SHOPPING

Florence is growing and new suburban neighborhoods are continuously expanding from the city center. Thanks to their convenience, one-stop super stores are an emerging trend along with covered malls similar to those found in North America. The most popular supermarket/convenience stores in or near Florence are: Esselunga, La Standa, Coop and Conad.

Central Florentine locations are listed below:

Esselunga
(This chain will also deliver, check out their website at www.esselungacasa.it)
Via Masaccio 274
Via Pisana 130
Via Milanesi 32
Viale Giannotti 75

La Standa
Via Pietrapiana 42/44r

Coop
Via Gioberti, near Piazza Beccaria
Via Cimabue 47
Via Gian Paolo Orsini 41 r
Piazza Leopoldo
Viale Talenti 94

Conad
Via dei Servi (near the Duomo)

Small specialty stores
Pegna is a small luxury supermarket located on via dello Studio 8, next to the Duomo.

Vivimarket, at via del Giglio 22r, has a good selection of imported products.

The English Store at via Vecchietti 28r carries numerous English specialty products like Cranberry juice, teas and toffee.

BUYING VEGETABLES AND FRUIT IN A SUPERMARKET

Italians do not like to see people handling fresh fruit or vegetables without some sort of 'protection'. When you enter a grocery store and head to the produce section, you are expected to slip on the plastic disposable gloves, provided next to the plastic bags. Select your produce and then take your selections to the scales located in the produce area. You are responsible for weighing each selection. The scales have pictures with a corresponding bin number that you insert. They automatically calculate the cost of your purchase and issue a small sticky label that you attach to each plastic bag. If you don't follow this procedure, you'll be very unpopular at the check out counter!

Tips for supermarket shopping:

Bring change: A one or two euro coin is required to release a shopping cart and is returned when you reattach the cart after you are finished shopping.

Una Carta Soci: When checking out at an Esselunga or Coop supermarket the cashier will often ask you if you have a '*carta soci*'. Although you don't require a membership card to shop at these stores, having one does provide benefits to the bearer.

Buste: Shopping bags. You'll be charged for each shopping bag you request at supermarkets. In Italy customers bag their own groceries; you may be asked how many *buste* you require or you may have to request them yourself.

Household Goods

Florence is famous for its wonderful shops for china, crystal, ceramics, art and antiques. Many are small artisan-run establishments where you can find one-of-a-kind purchases to enhance your collection of valuables. On the other side of the river in the *Oltarno* district near Santo Spirito, treasure hunters can visit artisan and studio workshops for wood, stone, leather, jewelry and fine arts.

Every neighborhood has its own hardware stores, which provide typical supplies such as nails, hooks, etc. You can rent power tools at some of these hardware stores. If you're looking for more extensive purchases of utilitarian merchandise there are several large manufacturers located on the outskirts of Florence. For cheap and cheerful household goods try IKEA, OBI and I GIGLI.

IKEA Firenze
Via Fracesco Redi,1
50019 Sesto Fiorentino
Call center: 199-11.46.46
Monday-Sunday 10am – 9pm

Centro Commerciale 'I Gigli'
Via San Quirico, 165
50010 Loc. Capalle, Campi Bisenzio (Firenze)
Tel: 055/8969250 – fax: 055/8969569
Hours: Monday-Saturday - 9am to11pm
Open the first Sunday of the Month

Bricolage Centre OBI
Via Petrosa, 19
50019 Sesto Fiorentino (FI)
presso Centro Commerciale Sesto
Tel: 055/448581 - fax: 055/4485844
Monday-Saturday: 9am – 9pm

TABACCHERIE: *the most useful mini stores.*
You'll recognize this useful shop thanks to its typical 'T' sign in blue, black or white. It sells all tobacco products as well as bus tickets, telephone calling cards, stamps, single envelopes and even lottery tickets. Although a mini version of the North American drugstore in many ways, Tabaccherie do not sell toiletries—you'll find those in a farmacia or pharmacy.

HOW TO BUY STAMPS
You can buy stamps, *francobolli,* at any tabaccheria or post office. A letter or postcard weighing 20 grams or less costs 41 cents for an EU destination and 52 cents when sent to the US. First class post, *posta prioritaria,* generally fulfils its promise to deliver within 24 hours in Italy, three days for EU countries and four to five days for the rest of the world. First class letters weighing 20 grams or less, costs 62 cents in Italy or any European country, and 77 cents outside the EU.

Outlet Shopping

Florence has decent shopping with most major fashion houses tenanting street fronts near the center around piazza della Libertà and via Tornabuoni. Those in search of a great deal should visit the several outlet shops near Florence that provide a wide selection of designer and ready –to-wear clothing and select merchandise.

Located in Incisa about a 20-minute drive south of Florence, you can find THE MALL. It carries a vast range of designer outlets including Ferragamo, Gucci, Armani, Valentino, Zegna (and many more, with prices approximently 20 – 40% less than those found in the city center. The selection is inconsistent but it's worth the drive just to see the elegant shopping center complete with a contemporary bar and small bistro. Shuttles leave from the city's main—check their website for more information at ***www.themall.it***

Driving Directions: Take the A1 towards Rome, Exit at Incisa and follow signs to Reggello Leccio. Via Aretina 63. Tel: 055/865775

Barberino Designer Outlet is located North of Florence heading towards Bologna at the Mugello exit. It features designer and high street brands in a faux Italian hill-top village setting. For information call 055/ 842161 or visit ***tourism@mcarthurglen.com***

Other outlets around Florence:

Dolce & Gabbana
Santa Maddalena 49, Pian dell'Isola, Incisa in Val D'arno
Tel: 055/83311

Fendi
Via Pian Dell' Isola 66/33 Rigaano Sull'Arno (Incisa Exit)
Tel: 055/83491

Prada Outlet: Space (the name used for the outlet store)
Loc. Levanella, SS 69.
Tel: 055/91901
　　A bit more difficult to find, I Pelletieri d'Italia is a farther drive south. Exit off Highway A1 south at Valdarno after Montevarchi. Expect another 10 minutes of convoluted town traffic before you reach their virtually unidentified warehouse space.

BP Studio Factory Store
Piazza Marconi 1, Sesto Fiorentino (next to Ikea)
Tel. 055/32361

Pratesi (Luxury linens)
Via Montalbano 41 - Casalguidi Pisotia.
Tel. 057/3526462
Take Highway A11 towards Genova, exit in Pistoia.

Roberto Cavalli Outlet
Viale Giulio Cesare 19, Sesto Fiorentino (near Ikea)
Tel. 055/317754

Richard Ginori Outlet
　　High end house wares
　　Viale Giulio Cesare 19, Sesto Fiorentino
　　Tel: 055/4210472

IVA (VAT) Taxes
Usually included in posted store prices, sales tax (IVA) is applied to all purchases and services. By law all non-EU residents are entitled to an IVA refund on purchases of 155 euro and over at shops that display 'Tax free shopping' stickers on their windows. At these stores present your passport when paying and ask the store clerk to issue you a 'tax free form' with your receipt. Often clerk themselves will complete part of the paperwork. You need to fill in your personal details and passport number.

In order to get the refund you must present your passport and all completed tax forms to airport customs (in Florence you'll find a small kiosk at the back of the departures check in area). It's best to have your unused goods available for showing (they don't always ask to see them but it's better to have them easily accessible). The refunds are provided instantly in either cash or credit in your choice of currency.

Note: Tax-free refunds are also handled in central Florence at the currency exchange booth, kitty corner to the north end of the Ponte Vecchio. They will charge a 10% fee for the service.

FINDS FAKES AND FINES
By Deborah Kennedy

No one's being fooled on the Ponte Vecchio

Like them or loathe them, **street vendors** are an everyday encounter on the busy streets of Florence. Whether in the main shopping streets or lurking on the corners of winding back streets, the traders ply their wares to tourists and locals alike.

Deborah Kennedy examines this intrinsic aspect of Florence culture and its impact on the local and national economy.

The street trader scoops up posters from the ancient, cobbled streets of Florence like a black-jack croupier; lifting the cards in one fell swoop–each tiny shard of stiffened paper falling neatly behind the other in his palm. The police have arrived. By foot on the magnificent Ponte Vecchio, by car outside the Uffizi Gallery, where they meander slowly towards the many traders—a wry smile on their lips. It's a game. The police know these men and women, mostly black, are mainly illegal immigrants; plying their wares to the awe-struck tourists who'll buy anything from the pavements of this historic Renaissance city. And don't discount the locals, after a cheap umbrella, as the winter rain begins to plummet.

The trader knows the rules, pack and run; run fast. Or, linger, make eye contact with the officers. Will they let it slide this time? For the bemused onlooker, it's like a game of tag. If the officers grab the trader, game over. There's no gentle warning in this tourist hub. But, as the police car pulls away, another trader replaces his street-space rival and the posters are back on the ground within seconds. Marilyn Monroe, Elvis Presley, James Dean and the occasional Botticelli copy. The handbags, the sunglasses, all fake, the rows and rows of gloves; laid out neatly again.

As the officers leave, they know that to look back is to roll the dice again. Maybe tomorrow.

Submerged, underground, black market. Call it what you will, but money generated from this form of labour in Italy is estimated to account for 20 to 30 per cent of the nation's gross domestic product. While trade has been the backbone of the country for hundreds of years, the influx of illegal immigrants to Florence and other cities in

Italy, from Africa, the Middle East, China and Latin America, is a relatively new phenomenon.

A United States Department of State report on human rights practices, released in 2004, said that the number of **illegal immigrants** in Italy increased by a whopping 43 per cent in 2003, as a result of legislation the previous year allowing a grace period in which illegal immigrants could become legal residents. However, integration and cultural assimilation have proven difficult, leading to an isolated and disaffected sub-society which relies on underground work or unskilled labour to make a living. Those who don't take their employment prospects into their own hands are often under protected and over exploited in the second tier of the illegal work force, which includes domestic work and hard labour.

Recently, the local government launched a crackdown on counterfeit merchandise sold by the traders on the streets, in an effort to protect manufacturers and fashion houses. Local producers are under threat from greater quality fakes which are becoming more authentic in appearance, allowing a whole section of middle income earning locals, as well as tourists, to wear the latest "Prada", "Gucci" and "Fendi" without mortgaging the Motto.

According to a recent report in the International Herald Tribune, nine out of ten fakes seized as part of the government crackdown so far have been taken from roaming vendors on the streets and plazas of Italy. However, for the busy tourist, stunned by the beauty of Florence from every vantage point, the street traders are but a passing curiosity; occasionally raising ire, if it's been a long, hot day, but equally capable of generating gratitude, if it's pouring with rain, or pelting snow and they're stuck without an umbrella, gloves or a scarf.

But for the economy and the future of Italian fashion houses, the impact of cheap, Asian-produced, high quality goods remains to be seen. Although one suspects that those who can afford Gucci and Prada and Fendi will continue to buy the real thing, while those who can't will simply continue to buy off the streets. A happy equilibrium which seems to work reasonably well, for now.

Article originally printed in The Florentine Issue 26 - Feb. 9, 2006

Ordering a Coffee

You can pretty much count on the fact that no matter how small or grand a cafè is in Italy, it will very likely offer you a good cup of coffee made from quality Arabica bean blends. Menus are relatively simple so don't enter a bar and start reciting the North American litany of over-sized caffeine beverage concoctions. In Italy coffee is a staple based on the essential extraction of rich flavorful espresso. It's served with or with out milk, or with varying degrees of hot water. Depending on the weather and season it can be served with ice cream or ice. That's it.

Lately in some Italian cafès, *baristi* have started to provide *latte scremato*, low fat milk, to accommodate North American trends. But beware that your specification may go unnoticed by the *barista* who may deliver you a regular cappuccino as he has done countless times over innumerable days to the unsuspecting foreigners. They innocently enjoy the flavorful beverage guilt-free with 'oohs and ahhs' a good cup of coffee deserves.

COFFEE TERMS

Caffe :	epsresso also known as caffe normale
Caffe affogato :	dessert dish of gelato drowned in a shot of espresso
Caffe americano :	espresso with extra hot water added to resemble American coffee
Caffe coretto :	espresso with a shot of grappa
Caffe decaffeinato :	decaffeinated (usually made with the grain orzo)
Caffe latte :	hot milk with espresso, served in a glass
Caffe lungo :	same as caffe americano
Caffe macchiato :	espresso with a dollop of milk foam
Caffe shakerato :	sweet summertime drink of cold coffee and ice shaken and served in a cocktail glass

Cappuccino :   espresso with hot milk and foam
Latte :   glass of milk
Latte macchiato :   hot milk with a dollop of espresso
Te :   tea
Te deteinato :   decaffeinated tea

Gelato

There are two kinds of ice cream available in the numerous shops of Florence. One is the classic, second to none home-made variety, *gelato artigianale*, and the second is the processed version of the dessert, *gelato industriale*. Though the latter is still better than most brands prepared in North America, it is made from a ready-made base with prepackaged flavorings and colors. The *artiginale* product is made from scratch using only natural ingredients and fresh fruit.

TERMINOLOGY
Tabaccaio : the most useful mini store.
Francobolli : stamps
Salumeria : deli
Fornaio : the bakery
Pasticceria : the pastry shop
Macelleria : the butcher shop
Farmacia : pharmacy
Ferramenta : hardware store
Pescheria : fish shop
Sartoria : seamstress/ tailor
Calzolaio : cobbler /shoe maker
Prezzi fissi : fixed prices
Sconto : discount

"Even now I miss Italy dearly, I dream about it every night."
— Eila Hiltunen

6 GETTING AROUND

City Transportation

Florence is a relatively small city when you consider its historic core. It can take only 30 minutes to walk from one walled side to the other. Florence's ancient winding streets have been preserved almost intact since its earliest days and cars are quite unnecessary. The best way to experience the historic center is on foot or by bike.

There are also small electric public buses that shuttle the weary, elderly and package-laden throughout the cobbled center.

Walking & Bike Riding

Most of the main sites and shopping areas in Florence are located within a 15-minute walking radius from each other. Women will need good shoes; either flats or wedge heels are essential. (Yes, you will see Italian women confidently striding on high heels through the mines of uneven stones but this is a skill learnt in early childhood. Equally amazing is to see ladies on bicycles— pedaling with 5-inch stiletto heels!)

Biking is a wonderful way to get around the city quickly. If you are a biker, you'll quickly become very skillful at maneuvering through crowds. Learn to adapt your senses to the sound of approaching cars and buses as they sneak up from behind. After a bit of practice and a couple of hopefully harmless falls, you'll become knowledgeable about the side streets less traveled by pedestrians. In the evening, when the pedestrian traffic thins out, there is nothing more liberating than riding a bike through the quiet streets of ancient Florence. For bike rentals and sales see: *The Essential White Pages*.

Bus Travel

When visiting Florence and other areas around Tuscany, the bus is often your best option. City buses serve the entire city and its outlying areas and are operated by ATAF in Florence. Bus tickets must be bought in advance from a *tabaccheria* shop, newsstand or any other store displaying an ATAF sticker in the window. A 60-minute ticket costs 1.20 euro and is valid for one hour on any number of buses. You can also buy 2, 3 and 7-day tickets. For a monthly ticket, you need to purchase a photo ID pass (see below). Once on board, punch your ticket in one of the machines on the front or back of the bus.

Students under 26 years of age are entitled to a discounted monthly bus pass that allows for unlimited travel on all ATAF lines for 20.70 euro. You can buy one from any ATAF vendor but to get one you must first apply for a photo card at the ATAF office outside the main train station at Santa Maria Novella (across from the McDonalds). Bring five euro, a passport-size photo and a document proving you are indeed a registered student.

Note: ATAF buses go to Fiesole, Settignano and Piazzale Michelangelo. Also watch for the smaller electric buses (A, B, C, D) which serve the downtown area. They come by almost every ten minutes and give easy access to the entire historic center.

The **Carta Agile** is a special electronic ticket which includes several bus-trips. It can be used by more than one person and its flexibility saves time by eliminating line-ups. This type of pass can be bought at a tabaccheria.

Iris tickets are all-in-one tickets for travel between Florence and Prato with several different coach companies. They are valid on urban buses, out-of-town buses, and with interregional, regional and direct trains. An Iris ticket holder enjoys the added benefit of discounts to select museums, theatres and exhibitions. It costs 8 euro for one day and 23 euro for a 3-day pass. Children travel with discounts. For more information see: ***www.ataf.net***

To visit other areas of Italy, such as the beaches of Viareggio and Forte di Marmi, check out the blue Lazzi buses that leave from the Santa Maria Novella train station. Their website is ***www.lazzi.it***

For transportation to Siena and San Gimignano, try the SITA buses, which leave passengers near the train station at via Santa Caterina da Siena 17r. Their website is ***www.sita.it***

Taxis

Taxis in Florence are worth their weight in gold—if you can find one. The city is often overcrowded and the number of taxis available doesn't effectively correspond to demand. Be prepared to wait quite a bit for a taxi, especially during the height of tourist season. One possible solution is to go into a hotel and ask the concierge to try and hail you one. When calling from your apartment or home, be prepared to pay an extra charge for door-to-door service. Expect extra charges during late evenings, on holidays or for extra luggage (even shopping bags). When it rains, finding an available taxi becomes a Darwinian race of survival of the fastest. Always carry an umbrella on potentially rainy days – taxis seem virtually non-existent.

Most taxis only accommodate four passengers at a time. Some vehicles can fit five people but you generally need to reserve them in advance. When entering a taxi, note that there will already be a standard fee of about 4.25 euro on the meter. In addition, drivers will legitimately apply an extra surcharge for out of town destinations or when dealing with early morning requests. The fee to the airport is approximately 20 to 25 euro.

Also be aware that taxi strikes are often called unexpectedly. If you plan on taking a taxi to the airport it's advisable to reserve a driver and car the day before your departure. If you do get stranded by a strike on departure day, head to the train station with baggage in tow. You can then get to the airport via bus.

To Call a Taxi: There are three taxi numbers: 055/4343, 055/4390 or 055/4242. You may want to try all three numbers and be prepared to call several times. Sometimes it may take two or three tries to get through, especially in the busier seasons or when the weather is inclement. You may be asked to *attendere in linea* (hold the line for an operator). A real person will eventually answer and ask for your name and pick-up location. They'll then tell you the name of your taxi (often a city name like Torino), the expected arrival time and a confirmation number.

Make sure you stay on the line until you receive this information.

You may also try heading straight to one of the main taxi stands located in several areas throughout the city: Piazza Santa Trinita, Santa Maria Novella, Piazza della Repubblica, Piazza Duomo, Piazza Ognissanti, Piazzale Donatello and Piazza Santa Croce. Keep your eye out for a stand wherever there are hotels and attractions. Note: you can try hailing down a cab though it's not always a successful technique.

Cars, Parking & Highways

Florence is not a very car-friendly city. It is small and congested and only locals who live and work in the city have car access inside the center's old Roman walls and towers. You will often find flustered tourists making an attempt to squeeze down one-way streets or across a piazza crowded with pedestrians. Nonetheless, the city center is off limits and there is signage everywhere to prove it. You can drive into Florence via several entrance points where cameras take a photo of your license plate upon entry. You are expected to make your way immediately to a public garage where you are allowed to park your car for an allotted period of time. Each garage is responsible for registering your license plate with the authorities so that you don't receive a fine in the mail.

If you live in the historic center and wish to park a car near your home, you may register your vehicle at Parcheggio Firenze on viale Matteotti 54 (Tel. 055/503021). You need to present yourself personally and should bring 20 euro, a valid driver's license, your car license number and a copy of your housing contract that states you live in the center. You'll be given a pass that you must leave on your dashboard at ALL times along with an electronic telepass that goes on the windshield. There are four areas in Florence A, B, C, D and you can enter, drive and park in your allotted area only. They will review all of these regulations with you directly at the parking office.

If you decide to have a car in Florence, it's advisable to choose a small model as the streets tend to be treacherously narrow. The same advice applies even if you just need a car for heading to the countryside for weekend jaunts. Tuscany's small hillside villages and lovely winding roads are better suited for the 'compact' than the 'compactor' and parking becomes much less tiresome.

Garages

There are several public garages available for those brave enough to venture into the Renaissance labyrinth. These garages offer limited daily parking at a premium of 25+ euro per day. The cost ultimately depends on the size of your car. Note that most garages are only open from 9am to 10pm and many are closed on Sundays). Essentially, if you enter a *zona controllata* as an unregistered car, you have approximately 15 minutes to register yourself with an approved public parking garage within the city walls. As stated, the garage will call the city parking authorities and register your license plate number so you will not receive a fine.

For a list of public garages see:
www.firenzeparcheggi.it

Private garages include:
Garage Angloamericano
Via Dei Barbadori 5 – 055/214418

Garage Bargello
Via Ghibellina 170/R – Tel: 055/287058

International Garage
Via Palazzuolo 29 – 055/282386

Garage Ponte Vecchio
Via Dei Bardi 35/45/R – Tel: 055/2398600

There are times when these restrictions do not apply, but as these rules change frequently, it's best to check with the city police. At the time of printing, drivers are exempt from the above rules on Monday, Tuesday and Wednesday evenings between 7:30pm and 10pm and on

Sundays. During these times, any car may venture into Florence and park in the center. (Note: certain piazzas and key attraction areas remain constantly exempt, such as Piazza della Repubblica, Piazza della Signoria, Duomo and Santa Croce).

If you do not have a registered car, you're not allowed to keep your car in Florence overnight. If your car remains in town after 10:30 pm, you may wake up to a 'clamped' tire, which generally results in a 150 euro fine and several hours of lost time. Traffic authorities will sometimes have cars towed to the impound lot located under the Pisa-bound Super-Strada on the outskirts of eastern Florence.

Should you find your car missing, check the towing lot BEFORE calling the Police. Should you find your car missing, check the towing lot BEFORE calling the Police. Their number is 055/4224142.

Be prepared to describe your car and provide its license plate number and the location where you left it. If your car has indeed been towed, take a taxi to the impound lot SAS S.p.a. on via Allende behind the Novoli market and report to the reception desk. You'll be asked to present your driver's license and a set of car keys. You must pay the fine in cash. Authorities will then direct you to your car.

If your car has not been towed, call the Police to report a stolen vehicle.

NOTE: In Florence **STREET CLEANING** occurs after midnight on a given day of the week depending on the neighborhood. If you don't move your car, it will get towed, so check the signs posted near the sidewalks for the specific cleaning day that corresponds to your street.

Auto Leasing

For non-EEC residents leases are best negotiated before arrival in Italy. A non-resident can lease a car for a maximum of six months. Leasing contracts can be renewed depending on circumstances. For a company that can provide you with all necessary documents, insurance and information, try KEMWELL at ***www.kemwel.com.*** They are located in the United States and their phone number is 001/207/8422285 or fax them at 001/207/8422286. Although the company is unable to deliver the cars to Florence, vehicles can be picked up in Rome, Milan or Nice.

It is also possible to discuss a private term lease with some Italian dealerships; in this case, the fee and terms are negotiated directly with the dealership owner.

Car Rentals

Florence hosts many car rental agencies including AVIS, EUROPCAR, PROGRAM, SIXT and HERTZ. Many are located near the train station on Borgo Ognissanti. Be sure to shop around for the best rates. As a rule, rental companies at the airport tend to charge a higher rate than agencies in the city center. Phone numbers and locations are listed in *The Essential White Pages.*

Note: Try asking about 'loyalty programs'. Auto Maggiore, for example, offers a program where clients get a discount after their third rental. This is a great program option if you rent occasionally rather than choosing to have a car full time. Service, prices and advice from the people behind the counters improve tremendously once you set up an on-going relationship with a company.

Car Purchase

Non EEC residents cannot buy a car in Italy. If you are considering buying a car, look to European brands from outside of Italy which provide foreign license plates so you can then drive the car into Italy. Most have programs which allow you to have the car in Europe for a year, and then includes shipping the car home. You can choose from many makes and models (with optional U.S.environmental and safety standards, if you want to sell the car in the United States). They cost less than their North American counterparts since European sales tax (which can run as high as 35%) is not added to cars bought by foreigners. All things considered, you can save enough purchasing your new car in Europe to pay for your trip -- and have money left over.

Almost any European car dealership in your country can handle the transaction for you. When you plan your trip, try to arrange to pick up the car and to leave it for delivery to your country in cities specified by the dealer. Volvos, for example, will be shipped free to the United States if you drop the car off in either London or Antwerp.

If you intend to resell the car in the United States, be sure to specify that your car be equipped to conform to Federal Motor Vehicle Safety Standards and to U.S. or state emissions regulations. If you get a car that does not meet these standards, modification costs will wipe out any savings you reap. Any new car bought in Europe comes with the same manufacturer's warranty as a car bought in your country.

The following European dealers handle cars built to U.S. specifications:

Shipside Tax Free World on Wheels B.V., Shipside Buildings, Kruisweg 631, P.O. Box 430, 2130 AK Hoofddorp, The Netherlands; (201)818-0400 in the United States.

This company operates showrooms and delivery centers at airports in Amsterdam and Brussels. l

Cars of Copenhagen, Vodroffsvej 55, DK-1900, Copenhagen, Denmark; tel. (45-3) 5-37-7800.

Iczovitz Tax-Free Cars, Claridenstrasse 36, CH-8027 Zurich, Switzerland.
This company sells the following makes built to U.S. specifications: Audi, Mercedes, Saab, Volvo, and Volkswagen.

Highway Driving

Italy is blessed with an extensive road system and its highways or *autostrade* criss-cross the country and make for fast and easy auto travel. Expect to pay a fee to use these highways. Smaller roads—generally one-lane scenic routes—are free. They are usually marked in blue or green on maps.

When taking an *autostrada*, drivers enter at toll booth areas, where an automatic teller provides distance cards. Take the *biglietto* and proceed to your destination. As you exit, the booth operator will punch your card and request the appropriate fee (cash only). Some toll booths have automatic tellers which digitally highlight the amount due once you insert your card. Place exact change *moneta* into the small mouth-like bowl and wait for the cross bar to rise. At some of the bigger exits, there are designated booths reserved for trucks and drivers who have a tele-pass and also for payment by credit card.

Special Note: Avoid the *autostrade* on Sunday evenings and during Italian holidays as highways transform into long winding parking lots. Plan ahead and opt for side routes or try to travel in the early morning or very late evening. Easter weekend and the time around *ferragosto* (the week of August 15th) are nightmare travel periods due to hoards of returning vacationers.

Getting Around Europe

One of the greatest things about Florence is its central position when it comes to getting around Europe. Not only does the train system provide an excellent network of easy getaways but air travel is easy and relatively affordable thanks to low-cost airlines.

Trains(Ferrovia dello Stato - FS)

Italy offers a decent level of train travel with a variety of passes. If you plan on using the train a fair amount while in Italy, it's worth going to the station and meeting with their information service to see what kind of a pass best suits your needs. Options abound: you can buy by time, by kilometer usage or according to the number of people travelling (family tickets). The Eurostar VIP lounge pass package gives several benefits, including discounts after a certain amount of usage. One of the best buys to be had is the *biglietto chilometrico a libera circolazione* which allows for unlimited travel in either first or second class. It is only available to non-residents, so you must show your passport upon purchase.

Italy offers several types of train services:
Eurostar/Pendolino = *intercity service, first class only*
Eurocity = *international express service*
Intercity = *national express train*
Espresso = *long distance express train within Italy, slower than Intercity*
Diretto or Interregionale = *slower than the espresso with more stops.*
Locale or regionale = *local service making all stops no matter how small – this is the MOST frustrating option!*

Locating Departure/Arrival Platforms *(Binario)*
When looking at departure boards for platform numbers *(bin)* be aware that intermediate stops may not always be listed. Double check the departure times of trains heading in your direction and watch out for your train's final destination such as Naples or Venice. Departure and arrival times are the key to confirming that you've found the right train.

Booking Train Tickets

The trenitalia website has a comprehensive on-line booking system that's easy to use. Once on board, you must present your e-ticket to the conductor.

When entering the ***www.trenitalia.com*** website, click the top right-hand corner to download the English version.

If you can't find what you are looking for on the website, visit any travel agency displaying the Trenitalia sticker on its window. Otherwise, head over to the information kiosk in SANTA MARIA NOVELLA station. Tickets can also be bought on site at numerous self-service machines and newstands in the train station. Remember to always stamp your ticket in one of the yellow platform machines before you get on the train.

Airports

Two airports serve Florence; the Vespucci Airport, also known as Peretola, has recently undergone a massive upgrade to accommodate its growing number of visitors. The most economical way to travel to/from the Vespucci is a 30-40 minute bus ride with the SITA bus or the ATAF city bus. Nonetheless, you should be aware that the city center is only 4 miles away from the airport and cab fare will only cost 20-25 euro depending on the number of passengers and baggage. It's about a 10 to 15 minute drive without traffic.

VOLAINBUS, a shuttle service connecting Florence's railway station with the Amerigo Vespucci Airport, is the cheapest link between the two. Shuttles run every half hour from 5:30am to 11pm and tickets can be purchased on board for four euro.

The second airport serving Florence is the Galilei Airport, located in Pisa—about a one-hour relatively direct drive. Taxi fare or private driver fees rotate around 50 to 75 euro. Alternatively, you can catch a train from the Santa Maria Novella Station directly to the Pisa airport. Do not take the one that goes via Lucca as it adds another hour to the journey!) Make sure you leave lots of extra travel time in case of late trains, traffic accidents or other unforeseen daily *incidenti*. If you cannot find a convenient train to or from the Pisa airport station, consider taking a short cab ride to or from the Pisa Central Train Station which has a more extensive schedule of trains.

Bus Transfers between Florence and Pisa Airport

There is a daily bus transfer service that goes from Pisa International Airport to Florence's train station and vice versa. You can buy tickets at the Pisa Information Desk located in the airport's arrivals terminal or at Santa Maria Novella's bus ticket booth.

For a complete schedule visit:
http/www.terravision.it.

Useful numbers:
Florence Airport Information: 055/30615 - 055/373498 - 055/3061700 - 055/3061702
Lost Luggage: 055/308023

Pisa Airport Information: 050/500707 – 050/849200 – 050/749202
Tickets: 050/582402
Lost Luggage: 050/849400 - 84940

Looking for Good Airfares

Most of us are aware of the discounted ticket options available through major suppliers like Expedia.com and Travelocity. Europe supports an unbelievable amount of small independent airlines offering incredible inter-European rates, so it's worthwhile to shop around.

For low-cost flights from Pisa to Dublin, Barcelona, Frankfurt, London and other destinations try:
www.ryanair.com

For low-cost flights from Pisa to Paris, Bristol and Berlin try: ***www.easyjet.com***

The Open Jet website (***www.openjet.com***) allows you to simultaneously search routes offered by seven budget airlines, namely BMIBaby, Easyjet, HLX, GermanWings, Transavia, Virgin Express and My TravelLite. All of these companies have their own websites, so make sure you cross check for other potential deals.

Other useful websites:
www.clickair.com
www.mobissimo.com/travel/search _airline.php
www.vueling.com
www.skyeruope.com
www.meridiana.com
www.virgin-express.com
www.basiquair.com
www.kayak.com

SCOOTERS

According to recent statistics, Florence hosts one scooter, or *motorino* for every five people living in the city. A practical way to get around especially if you live outside the center, scooters can freely enter the downtown area and are relatively easy to line up along the streets for parking. Drivers must be at least 16 years old and hold a valid driving license and permit.

If you plan on purchasing a motorino, be cautious about from whom you buy one. As it is not uncommon for stolen scooters to be re-sold with false numbers and permits, make sure the code on your permit matches the one listed on the motorbike. Depending on the size of the scooter, it is not considered legal to double up but you see it done everywhere. Riders must wear a helmet at all times. Though they are a fun symbol of freedom, scooters can be dangerous and are currently the number one culprit crowding emergency centers in local hospitals.

Before making your purchase you might want to rent first and see how you feel driving, parking and maintaining a scooter in the hustle of Italian traffic.

Stop. Lock and Roll
By Miriam Hurley
Cycling in the city

Florence is perfect for biking. Well, almost perfect. The center of town is flat. The climate is mild. The city is small and most points in Florence proper can be reached in less than 20 minutes by bike. Bikes free their riders from the plagues of bus strikes, impossible parking, blocked streets and high gas prices. They're fast, cheap, healthy and convenient.

On the downside, there are few designated bike paths or pro-cycling rules and amenities in Florence, discouraging riders from being faithful to the letter of traffic laws and making trips across town unnecessarily adventurous. There are very few bike racks, encouraging imaginative bike-parking solutions. And the city's pollution is especially hard on bikers. Getting caught behind a big ATAF city bus on a narrow street threatens to undo the health benefits of this form of transport.

Florence's long-standing problems with too much traffic and notorious pollution, which harms ears, lungs and historic monuments, could be much eased by more widespread bike riding. In the opinion of pro-cycling Florentine organizations such as Firenzeinbici and Firenze Città Ciclabile, it would take little to improve cycling conditions in Florence. Their mission is to pressure the city government to do that little bit. Cyclists ask for more bike paths, more bike racks, and city planning favoring bikes. This sounds much like what the city government promises. Deputy Mayor of Florence Giuseppe Matulli responds to those complaining about cycling conditions in Florence: 'This Administration has been working for some time to approve provisions that would favor the use of bicycles as an alternative to pol-luting transportation means. The primary objectives are to increase cycling paths, make new signage for bike routes, complete missing sections of cycling paths and improve and add bike racks.'

While we wait for these good intentions (presumably stuck in traffic) to bear fruit, biking is still the best way to get around Florence. Armed with a loud bell to get through tourist throngs, a hefty bike lock (essential for thwarting thieves who will always go for the flimsily-locked bike first) and open eyes, you can happily and safely make the streets of Florence your own. The rhythms and rules of traffic may differ greatly from your country of origin, so start out slowly. Keep your side vision well open and your hands near the brakes. Watch out for zealous taxi drivers. Keep visible with bright clothing and lights.

Finding the best routes to get around safely and quickly takes some trial and error. Using bike paths marked on a map (see www. florencebikepages.com) is a good place to start, though they are unlikely to take you all the way to your destination. A bike path rings the historic center; a good tactic for central targets is to position yourself on this path, which stretches from the Fortezza di Basso to the Arno near Piazza Beccaria, and find a spoke street to penetrate the center.

Bikes may not be parked on sidewalks or attached to poles. Naturally, with legal options in short supply, this rule is often ignored. As part of the recent Amo Firenze (I love Florence) clean-up campaign (which cranky cyclists suggested be renamed 'I hate cyclists'), many illegally parked bikes were forcibly removed and brought to an inaccessible lot where steep fines encouraged their owners to leave them forever. Under pressure from biking and environmental associations, officials now leave a notice on the bike before 'towing'.

Tourists can rent bikes from businesses such as Florence by Bike (www.florencebybike.com), by the hour or day. Second-hand bikes can be hard to come by in Florence. New, bottom-of-the-line bikes run between 100 and 150 euro. Reselling a bike at the end of a stay is easy by word of mouth or fliers. Florence by Bike sells bikes and will buy them back, for a reduced amount, within 120 days. Especially during the warm months, many cycling events are planned in Florence and Tuscany. For a list of rides, consult the calendars at any of the sites listed under "More Info". Through such rides, advocacy groups and dedication to human-powered transportation, cyclists are uniting to bring Florence that much closer to perfection.

MORE INFO:

Florence Bike Pages (in English)
Map of bike paths, places to rent bikes and
cycling events
www.florencebikepages.com

Firenze in Bici Association (in Italian)
www.firenzeinbici.net
Information on cycling advocacy and cycling events

Firenze Città Cicabile
www.firenzecittaciclabile.org
Information on cycling advocacy and cycling events

Article originally printed in The Florentine Issue 37 – July 13, 2006

The ways of the maze
By Suzi Jenkins

Via, Viale, Piazza

These are the Italian equivalents of Road, Street, Gardens, Avenue, etc. Fortunately for us there are fewer in Italian than in English, and by far the commonest are Via (street) and Piazza (square). The word street or square is followed by the name of that street or square; confusingly in Italy there is a standard group of names that are used in every single city and town the length and breadth of Italy.

For example, every town has a Piazza del Duomo and a Piazza della Repubblica plus a whole list of other names that would seem almost compulsory. These names tend to refer to historical figures (Piazza Garibaldi), or political ones (usually dead!) such as Via Aldo Moro. Favourites during Mussolini's times have Russian origins and are unpronounceable for the Tuscans that live in them! Possibly the most difficult of all are those roads that are named after dates; Via XXV Aprile, and Viale XI Agosto - and yes the numbers are all written in Roman numerals too, so if you don't know them, you are going to have to learn them all!

As to the numbers themselves, there is no rational 'explanation'. I will simply limit myself to telling you how it is. No questions allowed - it's like this because it is like this. Full Stop.

Odd numbers on one side of the road even numbers on the other. Sometimes...!

Large residences that have subsequently been divided, and indeed many modern apartment blocks, often have a single number for the entire 'single' home. This often means that six families have exactly the same address - you have to know the surname to be able to target the right one. Ah, yes, surnames. A married couple will have two surnames on every bell - the wife's and the husband's. If the wife's mother lives with them, then there will be three!

'Int.' next to the number means interno - an internal number, i.e. not an address that lies directly on the road in question. This could be a housing estate (rare in Italy) or it could be a small dead-end road that branches off the main one, and is not considered important enough to have its own name.

Letters are next to the number; very often house number 10 will become apartments 10A, 10B, 10C, 10D, 10E and 10F. This also sometimes happens on country lanes, where 200 years ago, two km of green fields separated number 12 and 14. Then in the 1960's when building laws in Italy were virtually non-existent, some property developer slapped up two homes in the intervening space, and hey presto, 12A and 12B were born! Then again, if number 68 further down the road had been destroyed by fire forty years ago, they could of course make use of that vacant number; 12, 68, 14!

And, finally, the greatest mystery of all. Someone, somewhere, at some time had the revolutionary idea of giving homes a black (nero) number and shops, offices and businesses in general a red (rosso) number (usually donated by the suffix "r") Beware; sometimes the numbers are actually written in those colours and sometimes not! So in the old streets of central Florence one side of the road could read: 2, 4, 2r, 6, 8, 4r, 10, 12, 14, 6r...get it? This is a practice that has been abandoned (how surprising) for new constructions, but the old roads still maintain it - and that is just about most of Tuscany.

Now slap all those rules together and a road whose numbers read: 117, 4r, 8B, 8D, 6r, 10, 22r, 16, 18A, 18C, 75 ...is no longer *a mystery! Right? Next we have the hamlet, village, town or city. Easy! It's where the house actually is, or the nearest collection of houses to it.*

A question you might be asked when giving your address, is the comune to which your house belongs. The comune is the town council that has jurisdiction over a certain area (much like a British borough) - so your house might be in Provinca di Firenze (Florence province), but Comune di Bagno a Ripoli borough of Bagno a Ripoli).

CAP - Codice di avviamento postale, the postal/zip code. The code for Florence is 50100 - this is a general code for the whole of the city; more specifically the house might be in 50127. The postal system does not rely heavily on the CAP and its use. Actually, we're not quite sure what the postal system does rely on!

That's it! Terribly simple once you know how!

Article reprinted from The Florentine - Issue 1 - April 21, 2005

For us to go to Italy and to penetrate into Italy is like a most fascinating act of self-discovery. Strange and wonderful chords awake in us, and vibrate again after many hundreds of years of complete forgetfulness.

— D.H. Lawrence

7 HEALTH AND WELL BEING

Italy has a socialized medical system and depending on whom you talk to the service is either said to be 'wonderful' or 'terrible'.

If you plan on using the system you'll require a health card from the Azienda Sanitaria. If you are employed in Italy, you'll need to present some employment information along with your passport and *permesso di soggiorno*. If you are not employed, you will be expected to provide your passport, *permesso di soggiorno* and records of your income. 400 euro per year plus a small percentage of your income normally grants you access to the health-care system.

Once you have your health card, you can visit doctors, dentists, eye doctors, hospitals, clinics and so forth. Although you'll sometimes have to pay a small co-payment for services, many types of prescriptions are covered. An emergency medical service is available for house calls. If you are using Italy's socialized system and need surgery, expect long waiting lists for non-emergency procedures.

In addition to the state health service, Italy has many private doctors, specialists and clinics. Italians and foreigners may choose to pay for private medical services and facilities in order to avoid long delays, enjoy better hospital accommodation or to obtain treatment from a preferred specialist. Some Italians and most foreigners purchase private health insurance, which ensures you receive the medical treatment you need, when you need it. If you are living in Italy without a *permesso di soggiorno,* you have no choice but to pay for private medical care and then be re-imbursed by your own insurance company abroad.

Italian Immigration generally requires non-EU citizens taking up residence in Italy to present proof of health coverage before issuing a permit to stay.

Medical Emergencies

Keep a list of medical telephone numbers next to your phone, including your doctor, dentist, local hospital and clinic, ambulance and other emergency services (such as the fire department and police). Emergency numbers can also be found at the front of all telephone directories as well as in the *Useful Numbers* section of *The Florentine*. If you're unsure of whom to call, dial the free national emergency number 113 and you will be put in touch with the relevant service.

Note the following recommended courses of action:

- *In a life-threatening emergency, such as a heart attack or serious accident, call the free public first-aid number **118**. State clearly where you're calling from and the nature of the emergency (see Italian vocabulary in this section for some assistance). Give your name and the telephone number. Don't hang up until the operator asks you to do so. Provided you call in response to a genuine emergency, you won't be charged for the use of emergency services.*

    - *If you need an ambulance, ambulanza, call Florence's service, Pronto soccorso ambulanza by dailing **112**. Most ambulances are equipped with cardiac equipment for emergency heart cases.*
- *If you're physically capable, go to a hospital emergency room or casualty department, pronto soccorso. All foreigners in Italy have the right to be treated in an emergency, whether or not they have insurance.*
    - *If you need urgent medical treatment outside of surgery hours and cannot get to your nearest casualty department, call the local duty doctor service or guardia medica at 055/2345884 or 055/215616. This service is usually available from 8pm to 8am on weekdays and from 2pm on Saturdays (and the day before a public holiday) until 8am on Mondays (or the day after a public holiday).*

- *If you need to see a physician but are unable to make the visit, a doctor will come to your home provided you call him during surgery hours. If he is away, his office will give you the name and number of a substitute doctor on call.*

In Italy it's an offence to offer medical assistance in an emergency if you aren't a doctor or qualified in first aid. It's also an offence not to assist someone in an emergency, i.e. by calling the appropriate service or by offering first aid when qualified to do so.

DOCTORS

Italy has the highest number of doctors, *medici,* per person of any country in the world—one for every 160 inhabitants. Not surprisingly, however, it's difficult to find English-speaking doctors in some areas of Italy, although most cities and resorts have a medical service for tourists, *guardia medica turistica* with English-speaking staff. Embassies and consulates in Italy keep lists of doctors and specialists in their area who speak English and other languages, and your employer, colleagues or neighbours may also be able to recommend someone.

Check the US Embassy in Italy website at <u>www.usembassy.it</u> for a list of English-speaking doctors in Italy.

General practitioners or family doctors are listed in the Italian yellow pages under the title *Medici generici.* Specialists can be found under *Specialisti* and according to their specialty e.g. *Ostetrica e ginecologia* (Obstetricians and gynaecologists). Note that the word *dottore* is also a courtesy title used to address any university graduate.

Private English Speaking Doctors in Florence:
Dr. Kerr is a private English doctor who caters mostly to foreigners. His clinic is located in the historic center at via Porta Rossa 1. Drop-in office hours are between 3pm and 5pm, Monday through Friday. Tel: 055/288055.

Studio Medico Associato is a private clinic that provides services from general practitioners and specialists around the clock. Staff speaks English and will make house calls, but you're required to pay in cash for all services. Tel: 055/475411.

Dr. Francesco Porro is a popular pediatrician with the English-speaking community known for his quick response to make housecalls. Tel: 055/474411 or 338/8203612

TOURIST MEDICAL SERVICES: if you require English language assistance during a medical emergency call: 055/212221

The Hospital Volunteer Service
This group of volunteer interpreters are always on call, ready provide assistance for emergency medical cases. Contact at time of printing is Laura Vezzosi at 055/4250126 or 055/2344567.

Dental Emergency
Open 24-hours every day, this service requires no emergency taxes. Tel: 055/241208

For a listing of doctors, dentists and other medical specialists *see The Essential White Pages*.

USING THE ITALIAN HEALTH SYSTEM

If you wish to take advantage of Italy's national health service, you must register with the *Servizio Sanitario Nazionale*. When registering, you're required to choose a *medico convenzionato*, or family doctor who works under a social security agreement. If you have children under six years old, you should also select a pediatrician or *pediatra*. You can get a list of available doctors from the local health authorities and can choose any physician willing to accept you as a patient. Each member of your family will be issued a personal national health number and a health card or *tessera sanitaria*, which you need to present when visiting a doctor or other health practitioner.

In addition to running individual private practices, many doctors also practice in group surgeries known as *poliambulatori*. Group practices can be private or state-run, operating within an Azienda Sanitaria Locale (ASL) building.

You can make an appointment to see a private doctor, specialist or consultant at any time, but you are required to pay. In Italy, many family doctors who work for the national health service also work privately as specialists. In this case, you will normally visit them at their private studio, *studio medico*, which may be separate from their state practice. To see a private doctor or specialist, you'll need to pay initial registration costs (around 20 euro) plus a fee for each visit, which can range from 40 to 160 euro. You will be expected to settle the immediately after treatment, even if you have health insurance. It's important to keep all medical receipts; they should be presented to your insurance company or can be offset against your income tax bill (depeding on your coverage).

Doctors' hours vary, although offices are usually open from 8am to 10am and from 3pm to 5pm, Mondays to Fridays only. Appointments aren't usually required and most offices operate on a first-come, first-served basis, so it's recommended to arrive early to avoid a long wait. Your family doctor will diagnose your problem and may write out a prescription or *ricetta* for you to take to the pharmacy. In addition, he'll arrange for you to have any necessary laboratory tests or X-rays at an authorized medical centre. When you need to see a specialist, your doctor will write a referral, *impegnativa*. Some doctors will make house calls, if you want a doctor to visit you at home, you must telephone during office hours (unless using a private clinic).

If you require specialist medical attention and want to take advantage of social security benefits, you must take your doctor's referral with you when you attend your appointment. Your family doctor may suggest a specialist, but you can also choose your own. Specialists registered with the SSN have their consulting room, *ambulatorio*, in state hospitals, local health authority buildings or other SSN centers. Some private specialists, known as *privati accreditati*, also treat social security patients at their private studios. If you have X-rays or laboratory tests done, it's your responsibility to collect the results and take them to your family doctor or specialist. There is often a fee associated with these tests.

If you're registered with social security, you must pay a subsidized charge with the cashier, *cassa,* so remember to bring enough cash with you. The cashier will provide you with a receipt which you then present to the specialist. If you need the services of a medical auxilliary, e.g. a nurse, physiotherapist or chiropodist, you also need a referral from your family doctor. Without the referral you'll be required to pay the full cost of all services.

HOSPITALS

All Italian cities and large towns have at least one clinic, *clinica* or hospital, *ospedale*, indicated by international signs which show a white 'H' on a blue background. Public hospitals are listed in the yellow pages under *Ospedali* and private hospitals can be found under *Case di cura private*.

In Florence there are several public hospitals :
Careggi Hospital is considered Florence's main hospital. It's north of the city center at Viale Morgagni 85. Tel: 055/79471111

Hopsital of Santa Maria Nuova is near the historic center, close to the Duomo. Tel: 055/27581

New Hospital of San Giovanni di Dio is located southwest of the city center, heading towards Pisa. Tel: 055/71921

Santa Maria Annunziata Hospital can be reached at 055/24961.

The Children's Hospital can be reached at 055/56621.

Private clinics:
Villa Donatello in piazzale Donatello: 055/50975
Centro Medico Omnia in Lucca: 348/2904608

There's a wide discrepancy between public and private hospital facilities in Italy, although many patients report little differences in the comparative quality of medical treatment. Private hospitals, many of which are run by the Roman Catholic Church, tend to offer a slightly more pleasant alternative to the sometimes minimal institutional facilities of public hospitals, but they don't necessarily have the most sophisticated equipment available. Some specialize in particular medical fields, such as obstetrics and surgery, rather than being full service clinics. Public hospitals have the benefit of a 24-hour accident and emergency department.

Be aware that few Italian hospitals have reception facilities and signs can be confusing or out-of-date so make sure you know where you have to go before you arrive. In public hospitals, all in-patient treatment under the national health service is free. For out-patient treatment, e.g. consultations, tests and operations that don't require you to be hospitalized, you will pay a fee. As for other medical services, a doctor's referral may be required.

The cost of hospitalization in a private clinic can be extremely high, ranging from 500 to 3,000 euro per day for hospital accommodation (including meals and medicines), plus the costs of medical treatment, e.g. over 5,000 euro for major surgery. The cost of private operations vary enormously depending on the reputation of the specialists involved and the fees they demand. If you have health insurance, be sure to check beforehand if you are covered for the treatment planned.

If the national health service doesn't cover you, you will be asked to pre pay for any treatment whether you have private health insurance or not, although some foreign insurance companies have arrangements with certain hospitals and may pay bills directly. You can pay in cash at the hospital registers, *casse* which are usually located in the main entrance lobby area. There are even atuotmatic tellers in some hospital lobbys that will take bank cards and or credit cards.

For alternative medicine: chiropractor, acupuncture, herbal remedies, see *The Essential White Pages*.

Pharmacies - *Farmacia*
You can recognize Italian pharmacies by either a red or green cross hanging outside. On a semi-official level, they function as mini clinics with staff able to give medical advice and suggest non- prescription medicines. Unlike their

counterparts in North America, pharmacies do not carry an abundance of periphery items; they provide medial and pharmaceutical products only. You will require a pre-scription, *ricetta medica*, from a local doctor to buy any-thing other than over the counter drugs. If you need an emergency prescription issued by a doctor you can go to the Misericordia in piazza Duomo—this Catholic medical organization is open 24 hours and it offers some free services.

Fitness and Spa

There are numerous gyms, palestre, pools and spas in and around Florence. Gym complexes can have any-thing from minimal exercise equipment and running machines to more luxurious facilities complete with spa services. In addition, there are several large new 'club' style complexes that provide a full range of sport facili-ties including racquet courts, pools, lessons and exer-cise classes. Most gyms and/or clubs require a minimum monthly commitment and membership fee but several offer a daily usage fee.

Italian Health Vocabulary

Aspirina:	aspirin
Raffreddore:	cold
Tosse:	cough
Crema:	cream
Pronto soccorso:	emergency ward
Influenza:	flu
Mal di testa:	headache
Salute:	health
Febbre alta:	high fever
Ospedale:	hospital
Indigestione:	indigestion
Infezione:	infection
Emicrania:	migraine
Antidolorifico:	painkiller

Ricetta:	prescription
Mal di gola:	sore throat
Sciroppo:	syrup
Dente:	tooth
Infarto:	heart attack
Osso rotto:	broken bone
Asma:	asthma
Taglio:	cut
Vomitare:	to vomit
Difficoltà di respiro:	difficulty breathing
Perdere coscienza:	to become unconscious
Dolore:	pain
Dito:	finger
Piede:	foot
Braccio:	arm
Mano:	hand
Testa:	head
Collo:	neck

"A man who has not been in Italy, is always conscious of an inferiority from his not having seen what it is expected a man should see."

— Samuel Johnson

8 BEING A TRAVELLER AND NOT A TOURIST

There is a great difference in being a traveler versus a tourist. Traveling allows for time, absorption, and thought. Tourists tend to take a birds-eye view of an area's top 10 to-dos and see list. Living in Florence provides first hand opportunities to experience the city, its attractions and cultural heritage at the slower pace of a long-term traveler. As a temporary resident you can avoid high tourist seasons, line-ups, crowds and agenda crunching.

Discovering Florence in smaller doses at your leisure is one of the greatest benefits to living in Tuscany. The marvels and beauty of the region's treasures become integrated into your daily schedule and interests.

Naturally there are the 'classic' things to do, like the Uffizzi, the Academia, the Bargello and all the guidebook type recommendations. However take time to discover your personal interests. Start with some of the walking tours to get a sense of the city.

This book is not intended as a guidebook as there are already a million of them, as well as articles, journals (blogs) and websites dedicated to exploring Italy. In the resource section in Chapter 10 are some suggested good reads about Florence and Tuscany. Many of these share new and less traveled areas to visit and explore, providing different and unique experiences. Familiarize yourself with adventures near and farther afield. *The Florentine* always lists a selection of special events, markets, theatre and destinations worthy of visits that are off the beaten track.

The hidden city
By Robert Nordvall

After you've seen the world-famous sites in Florence, how do you gain access to artistic treasures closed to the public? **Città Nascosta** *has the answer.*

Italy's artistic patrimony is the world's largest, but not all of it is on display. In 1994 **three Florentine women** — *Marcella Cangioli, Maria de Peverelli, and Tiziana Frescobaldi* — *decided to establish an organization in Florence based upon recently formed models in Rome and Verona. Their goal was to gain access to lovely places closed to the public, through small tours led by art experts. Thus, Città Nascosta was born.*

At first tours were held exclusively in private sites such as palazzi (Palazzo Corsini, Palazzo Peruzzi, and Palazzo Capponi) and other places, such as the Cloister of Santo Spirito del Carmine and the Rucellai Chapel. These early ventures emphasized the art of the 15th and 16th centuries.

From this modest beginning, Città Nascosta now sponsors about 100 visits a year in and around Florence that explore art through the Baroque period and even later. In addition to palazzi and closed spaces in churches, members travel to villas (such as Mondeggi, Ceretto Guidi, and Lilliano) and art exhibits in Florence and elsewhere. They venture to studios belonging to master craftsmen and contemporary artists, and seek out smaller museums off the beaten track of tourists. The excursions to Italy's lesser-known smaller cities such as Ferrara, Bergamo, Treviso, and Foligno are especially noteworthy for those who are already familiar with Italy's major urban centers. In the past, such towns were dominated by wealthy families who constructed magnificent buildings and were major patrons of the arts. Visits to cities beyond Florence, both large and small, are often made in conjunction with a significant art exhibition being hosted by the city.

The group's first event outside Florence was a trip to Rome in 1995. Excursions out of Italy began in the late 1990s, with a tour to Syria. Many of association's early foreign adventures focused on the cradle of western civilization in the Near East. Today, it organizes multi-day tours to major cities such as Paris, Prague, Budapest, and Berlin—all conducted by art experts hired by Città Nascosta, with the help of local art historians specializing in these foreign areas.

The group's **800 members** pay an annual fee of 12 euro. For this contribution, they receive separate schedules of tours for winter, spring, and autumn each year. The fees for individual trips, of course, vary. Città Nascosta cooperates with Associazione Dimore Storiche Italiane, a group similar to the National Trust in Great Britain and the National Trust for Historic Preservation in the USA. Each year, the Tuscan section of the association sponsors a garden day (**Toscana Esclusiva**) in major Tuscan cities, in which private courtyards and gardens are opened to the public. Entrance is free.

Under the sponsorship of the Ente Cassa di Risparmio di Firenze, Città Nascosta provides about **40 free tours each year** for Italian school students. As is often the case in cultural ventures, young adults are the most difficult group to reach. Tours are conducted in Italian, but most guides speak English well enough to clarify points for English- speakers with limited skills in Italian. By special arrangement, members can request visits in English, French, Spanish, or German. The group has branched into the tourist business by offering planning assistance and personalized itineraries for Florence that include access to residences, gardens and other locations not open to the general public.

Today a staff of five continues the work of the founders of this dedicated organization.

Città Nascosta is located at Lungarno Cellini 25.
The telephone number is 055/6802590
info@cittanascosta.it
www.cittanascosta.com Article originally printed in The Florentine, Issue 53, April 5, 2007

Pickpocket Prevention
By Sarah Beck

Florence is a relatively safe place, but as in every cosmopolitan city, petty crime such as pick pocketing and bag snatching is quite common. Happily, statistics show that reported incidents of pick pocketing in Italy have decreased by 11.4% over the last 8 years and bag snatching has been reduced by 22%. To ensure the safety of both you and your belongings it is necessary to be streetwise and use your common sense. This applies to students, tourists, foreigners and Italians alike.

1) *Make sure to weed out all unnecessary items from your bag, from your Blockbuster card to your now-foreign driving license, from photos of friends to any currency from home. All you need is a photocopy of your passport, student card, cash, one credit/debit card, mobile phone.*

2) *When leaving your apartment make sure your shutters or windows are firmly closed and all expensive equipment and important documents are out of sight. Lock the door behind you if you are the last one to leave; some of the spring locks in the doors require the key to be turned at least three or four times. Never attach your address to your keys.*

3) *Be wary of tactics to distract you. Dropped change, a spilt cappuccino or a beggar waving a cardboard sign in your face could all be tried and tested techniques to steal from you. Always have a good grip on your bag, with the zip front-facing and bags with long straps crossed lengthwise over your shoulder and body. Wallets should be kept in front or internal pockets, backpacks should be worn front-facing in busy areas and consider buying a small padlock as a deterrent.*

4) *When out in a restaurant, internet café, bar or similar don't just leave your bag on the back of your chair where you can't keep an eye on it. It's a good idea to slip the handle around your chair leg, wedge it between your feet or keep it on your lap.*

Should the unthinkable happen and something is lost or stolen, cancel credit and debit cards as soon as possible; replacements can be sent over in three to four days. Keep all the details and phone numbers in a safe place in your room. For lost or stolen passports get in touch with your nearest Consulate or Embassy here in Florence, Rome or Milan. To report stolen property in Florence go to the Carabinieri (military wing of the Police force) station in Borgo Ognissanti, 48. For insurance purposes you'll probably need a copy of your denuncia, police report, from the Carabinieri.

Article originally printed in The Florentine Issue 24 - Jan. 12, 2006MS

"What is the fatal charm of Italy? What
do we find there that can be found nowhere
else? I believe it is a certain permission
to be human, which other places,
other countries, lost long ago."
— Erica Jong

9 DAILY MANAGEMENT MANTRAS

Embracing Cultural Differences

A Learning Opportunity
In order to truly make your move to Italy successful, it's
essential to realize that things are not going to be the

same as they are in your home country. Daily life rotates on a different value system—not right or wrong but DIFFERENT. Take the opportunity to define life-style differences without judging them and accept diversity as part of the adventure of living in Italy. It's very likely that you'll encounter cultural challenges right from the get-go as you correspond with Italian governmental agencies, real estate agents, schools and employers. Therefore, when confronted with diversity avoid buying into derogatory stereotypical comments about your new temporary home. Instead, consider every surprise challenge as an opportunity to learn about a new culture. Ultimately, this attitude will contribute to your own personal growth. Be open minded, curious and empathetic. Undoubtedly, these are valuable qualities, particularly when living abroad. Most importantly, develop your sense of humor. Knowing how to laugh at life's trials and tribulations is a great tool when living in Italy.

A Different pace

When it comes to daily life, one of the first things you may notice about Italians is that they tend to 'march to a different drummer' in terms of pacing their time. While North Americans often value fast-paced active 'doing', it's important to consider that this is not necessarily a universally shared value. In fact, the idea of a slower, more relaxed lifestyle is what attracts many people to Italy in the first place. Those used to a faster and more aggressive tempo, however, may find the 'Italian pace' challenging.

Prepare yourself for the rythm of Italian living and take it into consideration as you plan your days. Accept pace as a cultural variable and use it as an opportunity to learn something about yourself, your environment,

history and people. Don't make the mistake of judging their pace as being unmotivated, or as proof of a 'manana' mentality. In reality, Italians work hard and stay on the job long hours but their work culture is structured and organized differently than in North America. In a word, they tend to appreciate the process. It has been said that Italians see life as a journey not as a destination.

Believe-it-or-not beliefs
By Nita Tucker

On political parties: Italy's varied history fosters a wide range of political beliefs and a huge tolerance for differing views on governmental and social topics. In this country, people are not afraid to be communist, socialist, anarchist or fascist. These affiliations are not demonized in any way. In an admission that would be unpopular in many other parts of the world, a former Cultural Commissioner freely stated that he's an active member of the Communist Party and that he had received his job thanks to this affiliation.

On patriotism: Modern Italy is not a patriotic nation except during the World Cup. It's a relatively new country that achieved unification less than 150 years ago. People prefer to classify themselves by city or region, rather than by virtue of national identity.

On the art of navigating: My friend Giovanni once told me 'Americans think the best way to get from point A to point B is a straight line.' This comment explains much about Italy—from the lack of signage on the highways to what makes Italians great lovers.

Essentially, Italians are not interested in the most direct route, they are interested in the most interesting route. They abhor boredom, so in order to be worthwhile, a process must be fascinating, challenging and open to many interpretations. Nothing is black and white. Shop schedules, for example, are a mystery. There is no place to go to find out which stores are closed on which afternoons and no set time at which they open.

Laws and regulations abound and a visit to the immigration office will leave you thinking that each official simply chooses the rule that best justifies his end. Personal relationships are essential to surviving and thriving in Italy. The art of navigating and negotiating is the key to discovering how to get things done!

On social trends: In Italy, Catholism and modern trends co-exist side-by-side. A Catholic country with the lowest birthrate in the world, its people have no problem with practicing birth control, having an abortion and still going to church. Many couples live together, have children out of wedlock, or are gay and still consider themselves culturally Catholic.

Some Do's and Don'ts:

Don't Complain
When things get challenging it's easy to be tempted to complain about differences. We all need to vent some frustration every once in a while, but avoid letting it become a habit. When you have a bad day, don't blame it on Italy. You had bad days at home, too.

Don't Culture Bash
As a guest in a foreign country, it is unrealistic to expect to always feel completely comfortable. If you were a guest in someone's home it's unlikely you'd criticize your hosts if they served you a meal differently than what you are accustomed to at home. When you mock, demean or criticize the culture of Italy you are, in fact, insulting your hosts.

Don't Be Agenda Driven
With the best of intentions, it's very common for people to set out a list of goals and things to see and do while living abroad. Many people strongly feel the added pressure of a limited time frame. Some days you may find yourself going crazy, trying to live up to all your self-imposed 'must do's'. Be wary of this destructive trend as it can add unnecessary stress to your time in Italy. Don't be too hard on yourself if you can't get through all your plans, instead concentrate on enjoying being where you are. Not every day has to be a 'do' day. Benefit from the advantages of the Italian rhythm of life, you'll find that taking time just to appreciate your surroundings will guarantee you a rewarding and truly authentic Italian experience.

Don't Compare Yourself to Others

Never compare your experience and purpose of visiting another country to those of someone else. Your agenda and motives are personal. You may know someone who has gone through a similiar experience or you may meet someone in Italy and feel that his or her time abroad is somehow more fruitful or exciting. Maybe they've learned to speak the language fluently or have made lots of Italian friends, took special lessons or had unique opportunities. Your time in Italy is YOUR TIME in Italy. There is no overall winner when it comes to this adventure, there are only participants—so be present to yours and enjoy!

Don't Just Socialize with Ex-Pats

It's natural to feel comfortable with people who share our native language and culture, especially when we are living in an unfamiliar environment. Making new Anglophone friends is wonderful, because your experiences will be enhanced by sharing theirs. Fellow ex-pats who find themselves experiencing the same types of adventures can serve as helpful resources to each other. Nonetheless, remember to make every effort to reach out and communicate with the locals. Try chatting with the man who makes your daily coffee or the waiter at your favorite restaurant. Talk to as many Italians as you can—you'll discover a warm, hospitable people who are proud of their country and pleased to share its many treasures with you.

Do's

Check your daily pulse

A sure way to keep on track and ensure yourself a positive experience is to take a personal daily pulse of where you are emotionally, mentally and physically. Acknowledge concerns, fears, dislikes and differences but also take note of life's positives by celebrating personal victories and accomplishments. Keep the experience real by making it a daily negotiation with yourself regarding your real needs and expectations.

Setting Goals

Goals serve as both guides and monitors which help us achieve personal success. Perhaps living in Italy has always been one of your major life goals. In order to successfully maintain and manage this dream, you need to map out a strategy, based on realistic action steps. Keep each step simple and attainable so you can build the momentum of accomplishments. The fact that you're reading this book suggests that you've already accomplished the goal 'to learn more'. Continue to set goals and create a daily or weekly list of what you would like to do or see.

Note: This is the opposite of the advice given in the previous section, 'Don't be agenda driven"...so obviously the challenge is to achieve a balance.

Networking: Try Talking to someone who's already done it

Research and reading are good methods to learn more about Italy and the opportunities it offers. Nothing, however, can take place of talking to someone who has already had the experience. There's no need to reinvent the wheel—if you know someone who has lived in Italy, talk to them and get their perspective. If a friend of yours has relatives in Italy...give them a call. Networking can provide wonderful resources for the future. Also take a look at some of the numerous personal websites and blogs on the Internet. See Chapter 10 for useful addresses.

Superstitious survival
By Roseanne Wells

Avoiding bad luck in Italy

You just spilled some salt: Do you throw another pinch over your left shoulder to avoid bad luck? Do you cross the street to skirt a black cat? When you break a mirror do you dread seven years of misfortune? The Italian culture has its fair share of superstitions and folklore. Just in case you're looking for luck in the bel paese, here are a few tips to keep in mind.

The trouble with numbers

Until quite recently, 13 was considered a lucky number in Italy—or was thought to be at least as harmless as other digits. According to Catholic tradition, however, there were 13 people at the table during the Last Supper, and Jesus was crucified on Friday the 13th. Thus, Italy has adopted the popular European belief that 13 invites as much misfortune as the country's traditionally unlucky number—17. The reasoning behind 17's stigma is twofold. If you re-arrange the Roman numeral XVII, it spells the Latin word vixi, a phrase often inscribed on tombs and gravestones. It translates as 'he lived' and is considered a sure-fire way to tempt death to come to your doorstep. The digits 1 and 7 also evoke fatal imagery—the one represents a hanged man, while the seven recalls the gallows.

Beware of the evil eye

Although not unique to Italy, belief in the malocchio curse is widespread in various Italian regions and especially prevalent in Sicily and the southern part of the peninsula. Known as the 'evil eye', this curse is considered especially dangerous for the young, the elderly and they sickly. The malady primarily stems from a nasty look but can also be transmitted via malicious thoughts—especially those based on envy or arrogance. Thus, in many areas, it's considered bad luck to tell a mother that her baby is beautiful. Such praise could breed rivalry and tempt the evil eye.

Special charms to ward off the malocchio include carrying chunks of amethyst or three pieces of rock salt wrapped in aluminum foil in one's pocket. But if the evil eye somehow glares past these precautions, the easiest way to remedy it is to rely on the gesture known as the 'horned hand'. Spread the right hand or both hands, palm facing downwards, and fold the thumb, third and fourth fingers in towards the wrist; then flick the index and pinkie away from the body. This gesture is said to pass the bad luck on to someone else. Better for you; maybe not so good for the next person!

Where the wild things are

In English-speaking cultures, we say 'break a leg' before a performance or big test, in hopes that by saying something terrible we'll somehow keep it from happening. The same idea applies in Italy: if you say buona fortuna, 'good luck' or tanti auguri, 'best wishes', before a pending exam, show or graduation, it's regarded as a major cultural faux pas. The proper way to guarantee success is to say in bocca al lupo, 'in the mouth of the wolf'. If one escapes the jaws of death, anything is possible. Just in case you receive these words of encouragement, the appropriate response is crepi, 'may it die'. If you say grazie, 'thank you', you lose your right to receive the good wishes.

Theater trouble

Although the superstition varies, actors and techies in the United States shudder if anyone utters 'Macbeth' during rehearsal or show-time, as it's taken as an ominous sign. In Italy, theater décor and signs are never purple, since that color represents theatrical disaster. Thus, actors always avoid wearing purple on opening night. Similar superstitions exist throughout Europe: the French are fearful of anything green in their theaters, while Spaniards are wary of yellow.

Home, safe home

Many Italians respect certain rituals and traditions regarding family life and the domestic sphere. Shiny new coins, heads up, on the windowsill before midnight on New Year's Eve bring prosperity.

But never put a hat on the bed; this superstition derives from when a priest would come to a house to give the Last Rites to a dying person and lay his hat on the bed. Strands of pearls are never given as gifts because they bring luck only if inherited. Similarly, gypsies believe that stealing pearls, coral or silver invites misfortune—everything else is fair game. Dripping oil on the floor is bad news, but spilling salt is worse and will attract seven long years of affliction.

Cin cin

It's both bad manners and ill luck to pour wine with the left hand. However, it's alright to spill wine on the table—a symbol of sharing among friends and company. Italians have a very specific way of toasting. When saluting during a toast, it's essential to look into the eyes of every person that clinks glasses. Cin cin, like the salutation 'cheers', is the most common phrase to use during these acknowledgements. And before the glass returns to the table, one must be sure to take a sip or else accept the bad luck that will follow if you forget.

If all else fails

If any of these unlucky things should happen, you can follow some of these curse-reversers. Touching iron can be applied to any situation. A bent nail kept in a pocket is also good luck, perhaps as an always-ready source of iron. There are charms that one can buy, the most prevalent being il cornetto, or little horn, which helps protect against all misfortune. But be careful: if you send negative thoughts to someone who has a cornetto, they will bounce back and afflict you instead. If the opportunity arises, leave your silverware crossed on the table; this is supposed to decrease any bad luck you've inadvertently acquired.

Article originally printed in The Florentine, Issue 56, May 15, 2007

Useful tips and good info to know:

When in Italy do like the Italians do. Making an effort to understand and adopt some of the common rituals and practices of Italian daily life will help you feel like an integral part of this dynamic and often colorful culture. Try and keep in mind this important cultural rule: Acceptance works where understanding fails.

1. Don't drink cappuccinos, lattes or complicated coffee drinks after lunch or dinner. To Italians, it is the equivalent of ordering a bowl of cereal after a meal. A small strong cup of espresso, *caffé*, is standard, though milk lovers can choose a *caffè macchiato*, with a dollop of foam.

2. Never ask for cheese on fish pasta, it's 'non si fa'.... just not done.

3. Whenever heading to the gym, dress in your regular street clothes and then change into your exercise gear once there.

4. Avoid walking around with open bottles of wine, beer or drinks in the streets and don't eat pizza and sandwiches on the run. Italians do not walk and eat unless they are at a fair or market.

5. It's customary to ask permission, *permesso*, when entering a private home, shop or business. Italy is not a self-serve society, thus it's customary to get clearance before sitting down in a restaurant, touching merchandise or crossing thresholds.

6. When Italians greet each other, they usually do the double cheek kiss, which actually involves 'kissing

in the air'. If you are uncomfortable with this form of greeting, always extend a hand to say hello or good-bye. *Buon giorno* works as a greeting until noon, *buona sera* is for afternoons and evenings. The informal word *ciao* is the hi/bye of the Italian language. *Arrivederci* means 'see you soon' and the slightly dramatic word *addio* (go to God) is seldom used unless your saying a good-bye long-term.

7. Restaurants often include a cover charge, *coperto,* for the bread, water and the tablecloth. *Servizio,* a service charge, is often included and usually implies a fee equal to 10% of the bill. It is not customary for Italians to leave a tip, but when service is good it's considered polite to leave a 5-10% tip for the server.

10 RESOURCE LISTINGS

Some Good Reads

The Collected Traveler: Central Italy (Tuscany and Umbria): Collected by Barrie Kerper, Three Rivers Press, NY, 2000.

Tuscany in Mind: An Anthology: Edited by Alice Leccese Powers, Vintage Books, NY, 2005

Buying a Home in Italy: David Hampshire, Survival Books, London, 2003

Living and Working in Italy: Edited by Graeme Chesters, Survival Books, London. third Edition, 2007

Gardens of Florence and Tuscany: A complete Guide: Mariachiara Pozzana , Giunti, Prato 2001

The Medici Villas: A Complete Guide: Isabella Lapi Ballerini, Giunti, Prato, 2003

Italians Dance and I'm a Wallflower: Adventures in Italian Expression: Linda Falcone, Florentine Press 2006

Florence, Venice and the Towns of Italy: Robert Kahn, Little Bookroom, 2001

The Antique and Flea Markets of Italy: Marina Aeveso, Little Bookroom, 2003

Made in Italy: A shoppers guide to the Best of Italian Traditions: Suzy Gersham, Universal Publishing, 2003

Insight Guide to Museums and Galleries of Florence: Brian Bell, Insight Print Services, Singapore, 2002

Florence, A Portrait: Michael Levy, Harvard University Press, 1998.

Florence, The Biography of a City: Christopher HIbbert, Penguin Books, 2004

The City of Florence: Historical Vistas and Personal Sightings: RB Lewis, Owl Books, 1996.

The Food Lovers Guide to Florence: Emily Wise Miller, Ten Speed Press, Berkley, 2003

Café Life Florence: Joe Wolf, Interlink Books, Massachusetts, 2005

More Good Reads About Italy
Under the Tuscan Sun: Frances Mayes
Bella Tuscany: Frances Mayes
The Hills of Tuscany: Ferente Mate
Italian Neighbors: Tim Parks
Italian Education: Tim Parks
Italy Out of Hand: Barbara Hodgson
The Agony and the Ecstasy Irving Stone

Useful Websites about Living in Italy as a Foreigner
Expatsinitaly.com
Lifeinitaly.com
Expats.org.uk
Romevillage.com
Usembassy.it
Britishinstitute.it

Useful Websites about Florence, sights, events and museums
Florenceart.it
Cittanascota.it
AboutFlorence.com
Intoscana.it
CommunediFirenze.com
Mega.it
Amicidegliuffizzi.it
Polomuseale.firenze.it
Firenzemusei.it (Museums in Florence)

THE ESSENTIAL FLORENTINE WHITE PAGES

This listing is a 'casual' compilation of information and services. It is by no means complete, nor do we endorse or warrant any of the individuals or businesses. We apologize in advance for any mistakes and/or omissions, and welcome your feedback and corrections.

If you would like to be included in the next edition of the White Pages, please contact us at info@essential-florentine.net.

Emergency Numbers
Other useful Numbers
Calendar of Public Holidays
Weather: Average monthly temperatures
Telephone references
Home Sweet Home
Help Sweet Help
Going Places
Healthy & Wise
For lovers of leisure
Where shopping begins
Sending your love
School Days
Museums, Galleries and Monuments
Embassies and Consulates

EMERGENCY NUMBERS

Medical emergency service:	**118**
General emergencies:	**112**
Police:	**113**
Fire brigade:	**115**

OTHER USEFUL NUMBERS

Police headquarters:	**055/203911 - Only to file a report**
International calls *24 hours a day:*	**170**
International Info *24 hours a day:*	**4176**
Telegrams:	**186**
American Express:	**055/50981**
Lost and found:	**055/3283942**
Veterinary emergency day service:	**055/7223683**

UTILITY SERVICE NUMBERS

Gas:	**800/862048**
Electricity:	**800/803500**
Water:	**800/314314**
Telecom:	**182**

TRANSPORTATION

Florence Airport:	**055/3061700**
National info 24 hr.	**055/3061702**
International info 24 hr.	**055/3061702**

Lost baggage:	055/3061302
Pisa airport (G. Galilei):	050/849300
Lost baggage:	050/849400
Railways:	892021
www.trenitalia.com	
Radio Taxi:	055/4390
	– 055/4242
	– 055/4798
	– 055/4499
Bus lines Lazzi:	055 363041
Bus lines SITA:	055 47821

MEDICINE AND HEALTH:

Careggi Hospital:	055/79471111
Hospital of S. M. Nuova:	055/27581
Children's Hospital:	055/56621
New Hospital S. G. di Dio:	055/71921
S. M. Annunziata Hospital:	055/24961
Tourist medical service:	055/212221
English-speaking doctors :	*www.usembassy.it*
Dental emergency:	055/241208
Studio Medico Associato:	055/475411
Pharmacy Comunale:	055/216761
Central Train Station:	
Pharmacy Molteni:	055/289490
Pharmacy all'Insegna del Moro:	055/211343

RELIGIOUS SERVICES

Santa Maria del Fiore:	055/294514
Santissima Annunziata:	055/266181
Baptist Church:	055/210537

Jewish Synagogue: **055/245252**
Shir Hadash Jewish
reform/progressive congregation: **348/6913059 or**
                                       348/9362564
Lutheran Church: **055/2342775**
St. James American Church: **055/294417**
St. Mark's Church of England: **055/294764**

CONSULATES

Great Britain: **055/284133**
USA: **055/266951**

PUBLIC HOLIDAYS

Jan. 1: *Capodanno* - New Year's Day

Jan. 6: *La Befana* – the Epiphany

Variable: *Pasqua* – Easter

Variable: *Pasquetta* – Easter Monday

Apr. 25: *Festa della liberazione* - Liberation Day

May 1: *Festa dei lavoratori* – Labor day

Jun. 2: Festa della Repubblica – Commemoration of Italy becoming a Republic

Jun. 24: *Festa di San Giovanni* – St. John the Baptist - Florence's patron saint's day

Aug. 15: *Festa dell'assunzione, Ferragosto* - Feast of the Assumption

Nov. 1: *Tutti Santi,* All Saints' Day

Dec. 8: *Festa dell'Immacolata* - Immaculate Conception

Dec. 25: *Natale* - Christmas Day

Dec. 25: *Festa di San Stefano* – Saint Steven's Day

Also note that Florence empties out when people disappear to the sea or mountains for most of August, shops are closed for holiday (*chiuso per ferie*).

WEATHER

Average monthly temperatures

	High	Low
Jan.	50°F	30°F
Feb.	54°F	34°F
Mar.	59°F	41°F
Apr.	68°F	46°F
May	75°F	52°F
Jun.	84°F	57°F
Jul.	93°F	64°F
Aug.	90°F	57°F
Sept.	82°F	55°F
Oct.	73°F	52°F
Nov.	61°F	39°F
Dec.	55°F	39°F

Telephone References

English Yellow Pages

Available at Florence's main bookshops and online www. englishyellowpages.it, it lists English-speaking services and useful numbers.

Useful international telephone codes

Country Codes

Albania	0355
Australia	061
Austria	043
Belgium	032
Canada	001
France	033
Germany	049
Hungary	036
Ireland	0353
Italy	039
Japan	081
Romania	040
Spain	034
UK	044
USA	001

HOME SWEET HOME

Accomodations (Apartment and home rentals, sales, and relocation services)

Knight Frank
Tel: 055/238457
www.knightfrank.com

Colours of Tuscany
Judieanne Colusso
Tel: 335/8390712
www.coloursoftuscany.com

Pitcher & Flaccomio
Tel: 055/2343354
www.pitcherflaccomio.com

Best in Italy
Tel: 055/223064
www.thebestinitaly.com

Windows on Italy
Tel: 055/268510
www.windowsonitaly.com

Home in Florence
Tel: 348/3813467
www.homeinflorence.com

HELP SWEET HELP

Legal Services - Lawyers

Andrea Davis
Via B. Lupi 14
Tel: 055/496014
mandavlaw@mandavlaw.it
www.mandavlaw.it

Vincent E. Lualdi
Piazza Indipendenza 21
Tel: 055/480055
lualdi@internationallawstudio.com
www.internationallawstudio.com

Carlo Mastellone

Viale S.Lavagnini 13
Tel: 055/4620041
eulex.network@studiomastellone.it
www.studiomastellone.it

Alessandro Bianchini
Tel: 055/2658111
Al.bianchini@tiscalinet.it

Accounting

Alessandro Marino Borraccino
Via nove febbraio, 2
Tel: 055/4634880
a.borraccino@tiscali.it

Andrea Corsini
Andrea.corsini@studiocorsini.it
055 2469165

Babysitting Services

Saint James Nursery

The local American Church has a group of reliable young women who can provide babysitting service short or long-term. They can be contacted through their website at www.stjamesnursery.com or call the church at 055/294417.

Agenzia Help
Via Bolognese 4r
Tel. 055/470333
For various services, cleaning, babysitter, etc.

Agency Euro-pair
Via Ghibellina 96r
Tel. 055/242181

TECHNOLOGICAL LIFE-SAVERS

Internet Points

Internet Train
Via dei Benci 36r, via Zannoni 1r, Borgo San Jacopo
30r, via dell'Oriuolo 40r
www.internettrain.it

Nettyweb
Via Santo Spirito 42r
Tel. 055/2654549
www.nettyweb.com

The Netgate
Via Sant'Egidio 14r, via Nazionale 156r, via dei
Cimatori 17r, via dei Serragli 76r,
Santa Maria Novella Station
www.thenetgate.it

Intotheweb
Via dei Conti 23r
Tel. 055/2645628

Webpuccino
Piazza Madonna
Tel. 055/2776469
www.campustelecom.it

Computers and Accessories

Data Port Macintosh
Viale Guidoni 173
Tel: 055/4220433

Imperial
66 via Erbosa
Tel: 055/689998

Mediaworld
Viale Pietro Nenni
Tel: 055/7371111

SMA
Viale Gramsci 8/10 r
Tel: 055/2260647

Brain Technology Spa
Via Francesco Datini 9r
Tel: 055/6810824

Computer Discount
Viale Francesco Redi 155
Tel: 055/334139

Computer Services

Tuscany Pc Clinic
Www.tuscanypcclinic.com
Tel. 334 1085438

Computer SOS
Tel. 320 0932811

HELP SWEET HELP

Plumbers

New Service Express
Tel: 347/8051604
www.newserviceexpress.com

Agresti & Agresti
Tel: 055/2049584
www.agrestieagresti.it

S.O.S. Casa
Tel: 055/434030

Electricians

New Service Express
Tel: 347/8051604
www.newserviceexpress.com

Italia Impianti
Tel: 055/666766
www.italia-impianti.com

Movers and Storage

Casaforte
Tel: 055/7327407
www.casaforte.it

Traslochi La Freccia Fiorentina
Tel: 055/7323593
www.frecciafiorentina.it

Traslochi Nuovo sole
Tel: 055/490078
www.traslochinuovosole.it

Bollinger International Movers
Tel: 055/4251086
www.bolliger.it

GOING PLACES

Car Rentals

Avis
Borgo Ognissanti 128r, Santa Maria Novella
Tel: 055/213629
www.avisautonoleggio.it

Europcar
Borgo Ognissanti 53-5, Santa Maria Novella
Tel: 055/290438

Program
Borgo Ognissanti 135r
Tel: 055/282916
www.programautonoleggio.com

Hertz
Via Maso Finiguerra 33
Tel: 055/2399205
www.hertz.it

Sixt
Via il Prato 80r
Tel: 055 301 283
www.e-sixt.it

Bicycles/ Scooter Rentals

Alinari
Via Guelfa 85r, San Lorenzo
Tel: 055/280500
www.alinarirental.com

Free Bike

This service, sponsored by the municipality allows you to use the Florence bikes for free.
For further information 055/5000453 - Mr Fini, 055/5001994.

Florencebybike
Via San Zanobi, 120/r
Tel: 055/488992
www.florencebybike.it

Car Services

Autofficina Inglese
Via Cittadella 6/r
Tel: 055/355693

Elettrauto Arno
Via Ponte alle Mosse 13/r
Tel: 055/332380

HEALTHY AND WISE

Medical Services

Tourist Medical Service
Via Lorenzo Il Magnifico 59
Tel: 055/4754 11

Istituto Ortopedico Toscano P. Palagi
Viale Michelangelo 41
Tel: 055/658 81

Ospedale Careggi
Viale Pieraccini 17
Tel: 055/4277111

Ospedale Santa Maria Nuova
Piazza Santa Maria Nuova 1
Tel. 055/27581

Centro Italiano Fertilità e Sessualità
Gynecological and infertility treatments
Via della Fortezza 6
Tel: 055/470521
www.cifs.it

Doctors

Dr. Stephen Kerr
General practitioner
Via Porta Rossa 1
Tel. 055/288055 or 335/8361682
www.dr-kerr.com

Anthony McDougall
Chiropractor
Piazza Stazione 1
Tel. 055 280212
mineofedi@libero.it

Dr. Porro
Pediatrician (makes house calls)
Tel: 338/8203612

Centro Oculistico
Eye doctor
Dr Valerio Grandi
Via Fossombroni 2°

Homeopathic doctors
Via Villari, 14
Tel: 055/678143

Dr Georgios Foukis
Esthetic plastic surgeon – medical clinic skin
Tel: 055/9061616 or 328/8523276
www.skinaestheticlinic.com

HEALTHY AND WISE

Private clinics

Prof. Manfredo Fanfani
Research clinic with English-speaking staff
Piazza della Indipendenza 18b
Tel: 055/49701
info@istitutofanfani.it

Istituro Prosperus
General surgery, Gynecology, Radiology, Cardiology,
Plastic Surgery
Via Cherubini 8
Tel: 055/527556
villacherubini@prosperus.it

Villa Donatello
Piazza Donatello 14
Tel: 055/50975
www.villadonatello.it
info@villadonatello.it

Ayurvedic Health Care

Ambrosia Ayurveda
Via Ricasoli 55/r
Tel: 055 283 830
Email: ambrosia@hesp.it
www.ambrosia.it

Dentists

Dr.NicolaPaoleschi
Tel. 055/241208
24 hours emergency: 335/8366567
www.studiopaoleschi.it

Studio Dentistico Miglietta
Via Fabbroni 57
Tel. 055/488354

Dental emergency.
Dr. Cristina Magnani
Via Matteotti 11
Tel: 055/578357

HEALTHY AND WISE

Veterinarians

Veterinarians at Your Service
Tel. 333/8005343 .
www.veterinarioadomicilio.com

Clinica Poggetto
Via Celso 4r
Tel: 055/473009

Dr. Tanzini
Via Cimabue 9
Tel: 055/242789

Ambulatorio Veterinario Masaccio
Viale Gramsci 65
Tel: 055/2347577

Ambulatorio Veterinario Notturno
Via R. Giuliani 214°/B
Tel: 055/4221194

All Night Pharmacies

Farmacia all'Insegna del Moro
Piazza San Giovanni 20r, near the Duomo
Tel:055/211343

Farmacia Comunale no.13
Inside the Santa Maria Novella train station
Tel: 055/216761

Farmacia Molteni
Via Calzaioli, 7r
Tel: 055/215472

FOR LOVERS OF LEISURE

Sports

Federazione Italiana Baseball/Softball
Via Barbacare 17
Tel: 055/4625127
Viale Milton 3
Tel: 055/4625100

Federazione Ginnastica d'Italia
Gymnastics
Via Malta 4
Tel: 055/671115 - 055/670233

Scuola Calcio Ferruccio Valcareggi

Soccer
Via Gignoro
Tel: 055/611014

Judo, Yoga, Gymnastics: Kosen
Via Confalionieri 20
Tel: 055/571809

FOR LOVERS OF LEISURE

Clubs (Social, English-speaking)

Garden Club
Via San Firenze 2
Tel: 055/282245

American International League of Florence Onlus

C.P. 130, Bagno a Ripoli
www.ailoflorence.org

Network
c/o Syracuse University, Piazza Savonarola, 15
wicks@katamail.com.

Firenze Moms 4 Moms Network
Tel: 333/5728945
www.firenzemoms4moms.net

Gyms:

Klab Wellness Center
Via G.B. Lulli 62
Tel: 055/333621
Phone: 055/333230
www.klab.it

Stadio
Viale Maratona, 6
Tel: 055/572398

Swam
Via dei Pepi, 28
Tel: 055/240802

Time Out
Via Ponte Sospeso 6
Tel: 055/714069

Tropos
Via Orcagna, 20/a
Tel: 055/678 381 - 661581
www.troposclub.it

Vivarium
Via Accursio 4/r
Tel: 055/2047471 - 2320059
www.vivariumcenter.com

Virgin Active
Via Dalla Chiesa Generale Carlo Alberto 11
Tel: 055/6504587

FOR LOVERS OF LEISURE

Horseback Riding

Associazione Italiana Quarter Horse
Via D'orso 13
Tel: 055/2120377 – 055/6120378

Centro Ippico Toscano
School for Riding and Club House
Via dei Vespucci 5/a t
Tel: 055/373721
into@centroippicotoscano.it

Ducci s.r.l.
Lgarno Corsini 24r.
Tel: 055214550

Bookstores

Paperback Exchange
Via delle Oche, 4R
Tel: 055/293460

Mcrae Bookstore
Via dei neri 30
Tel: 055/2382456

Feltrinelli international
Via Cavour 12r
Tel: 055/219524

BM Bookshop
Borgo Ognissanti, 4r
Tel: 055/294575

Edison
Piazza della Republica 27r
Tel. 055/213110

English-speaking Cinema

Odeon Cinehall
Piazza Strozzi
Tel: 055/214 068
Original Sound films on Mondays, Tuesdays and Thursdays
Shows: 4:30pm – 6:35pm – 8:40pm – 9pm – 10:45

British Institute
Wednesday nights
Lungarno Guicciardini 9
Tel: 055/267781
www.britishinstitute.it

FOR LOVERS OF LEISURE

Dance and music

Scuola di Danza
Via G. Fabroni 60-62r
Tel: 055/484210
www.scuola-di-danza-firenze.it

Alambrado Danza
Via Gran Bretagna, 189
Tel: 055/6812578

Max Ballet Academy
Via Landini 9
Tel: 055/331816

Florence Gospel Choir School
Via Campo d'Arrigo 44
Tel: 055/667674

Scuola di Musica
Via delle Porte Nuove 53
Tel: 055/322994

Centro Danza e Movimento.
Borgo. Albizi 16
Tel: 055/243008
www.centrodanzamovimento.it

FOR LOVERS OF LEISURE

Tourist Points

Agenzia per il Turismo
Via Camillo Cavour 1r
Tel: 055/290832
Via Alessandro Manzoni 16
Tel: 055/23320
www.firenze.turismo.it

Ufficio Informazioni Turistche
Piazza della Stazione 4
Tel. 055/212245
Borgo Santa Croce 29r
Tel: 055/2340444
www.comune.firenze.it
Consorzio Informazioni Turistiche Alberghiere
Santa Maria Novella train station
Tel: 055/282893

Museum Membership
To apply online for your membership at www.ami-cidegliuffizi.com

Tours

A.G.A. - Tourist Guide Association Florence and its Province
Via G.F. Mariti 8
Tel: 055/4486971.

A.G.T. Association of Tuscan Guides
Via Ghibellina 117/r
Tel: 055/2645217.

Associazione guide turistiche fiorentine
Via Ugo Corsi 25
Tel: 055/4220901

Florenceguides.com
Inspiring and entertaining walking tours in the Renaissance splendour of Florence, Italy with highly-qualified, professional, and fully-licensed tour guides.

Florenceguide.it
Guided tours in Florence and Fiesole for groups, families and individuals.

WHERE SHOPPING BEGINS

Markets

Mercato Centrale di San Lorenzo
Open 7am - 2pm - Monday to Saturday. Some stands are open 4pm - 8pm Saturday.

(Mornings only for the food market - Outdoor market stays open until the evening.) Florence's largest market is comprised of an indoor food market as well as a myriad of outdoor street vendors - many who specialize in leather goods. This centrally located, covered two-floor building has butcher shops, delis, specialty shops and grocer's on the main floor. Upstairs, you'll find fruit and vegetable stalls. The outdoor market hosts an array of Florentine wares such as leathers, paper products and souvenir items in addition to clothes, shoes and luggage.

Il Porcellino
Via Porta Rossa

8am - 7pm, daily. 3pm - 7pm, Mondays. Closed Sundays.

This centrally located market is primarily a 'tourist' market where visitors purchase leather purses, scarves, and specialty souvenirs from Florence. Most of the products here can also be found at San Lorenzo.

Mercato delle Cascine
Viale Lincoln, Cascine Park

8am - 1pm, Tuesdays

A large market that runs alongside the Arno river, the Cascine offers a large selection of clothes, shoes, produce, flowers and household goods. It's a good market to find a 'deal' away from the bustle of the more touristy market of San Lorenzo.

Mercato Santo Spirito
8am - 1pm - Monday to Saturday.

A small daily market, Santo Spirito offers limited produce alongside stands selling household goods and clothing.

Mercato di Sant'Ambrogio
Piazza Ghiberti

8am - 3pm. Closed Sunday.

A very popular market populated by local Italians, Sant'Ambrogio is a key spot to shop for daily groceries. Inside the covered building you'll see a wide selection of food items—butcher's, cheese and pasta makers and bakeries. Under the metal roof extension the market hosts a limited selection of household goods, flowers and some clothing.

Mercato dei Fiori
Via Pellicceria

Open 9am - 6pm, Thursdays.

Find fresh bouquets and plants under the arcade in via Pelliceria right in front of Piazza della Repubblica's central post office.

Mercato delle Pulci
Piazza dei Ciompi

9am - 7pm, Closed Sundays.

An eclectic mix of 'antique' shops gathered under a permanent structure. On the last Sunday of every month the market expands to feature a mix of vendors who line the surrounding street and bring an assortment of used and 'antique' goods including art, furniture, jewelry and clothes.

Outlets

The Mall
Via Europa 8, Leccio Reggello
Tel: 055/8657775

Dolce & Gabbana
S. Maria Maddalena 49; Pian dell'Isola Rignano Sull'Arno
Tel: 055/8331300

Robert Cavalli
Via Volturno 3, Sesto Fiorentino
www.robertocavallioutlet.it

Prada Outlet
Località Levanella, SS 69, Montevarchi (Arezzo)
Tel: 055/91901

Barberino Outlet
www.barberino.mcarthurglen.it
Tel: 333/8005343

SENDING YOUR LOVE

Shipping options

Central Post Office
Via Pellicceria 3, near the Duomo
www.poste.it

DHL
Via della Cupola 243
Tel. 800/345345
www.dhl.it

FedEx
Via Gobetti 3 - Capalle
Tel. 800/123800
www.fedex.com

MailBoxes Etc.
Here are the several locations in Florence.
Lungarno Guicciardini 11r - Tel: 055/212022
Corso Tintori 39r - Tel: 055/2466660;
Via della Scala 13r - Tel. 055/268173
Via San Gallo 26r - Tel: 055/4630418

YVO
Express shipping anywhere in the world.
Piazza Pitti 7/8r
www.yvo.it

Fracassi Worldwide Shipping
Specialized in art & antiques packaging and delivery.
Via Santo Spirito, 11
Tel. 055/283597
fracassi@fracassishipping.com
www.fracassishipping.com

SCHOOL DAYS

International Schools

The International School of Florence
Junior School (Pre-School to Grade 5)
Villa le Tavernule, Via del Carota 23/25
50012 Bagno a Ripoli (FI), Italy
Tel: 055/6461007
admin.tav@isfitaly.org

The International School of Florence
Middle and Upper Schools (Grades 6 to 12)
Villa Torri di Gattaia, Viuzzo di Gattaia, 9
50125 Florence, Italy
Tel: 055/2001515
admin.gat@isfitaly.org

Westminister International School
Via di Goletta 1
Tel: 050/2200754
www.westminsterinternationalschool.org

Fashion Schools

Accademia Italiana
Academic and Master Courses at University Level
Piazza Pitti 15
Tel: 055/284616 – 055/211619
www.accademiaitaliana.com
modaita@tin.it

Polimoda - Fashion Institute of Technology
Via Pisana 77
Tel: 055/739961
www.polimoda.com

Art Schools/Performing Arts

Le Arti Orafe
Via del Campuccio 8
Tel: 055/2280163

Istituto Lorenzo de Medici
Via Faenza 43
Phone: 055/287360

Accademia Bartolomeo Cristofori (music)
Weekly workshops for musicians and piano tuners
in spring
Via di Camaldoli, 7/r
Tel: 055/221646 – 055/2280010
La Bottega Teatrale (theater)
Borgo San Frediano 35 Firenze.

SCHOOL DAYS

Universities (accredited)

Università degli studi di Firenze
Piazza San Marco 4
Tel: 055/27571
www.unifi.it

Accademia di belle arti di Firenze
Via Ricasoli 66
Tel: 055/215449
www.accademia.firenze.it

Fairfield University
www.fairfield.edu/sce/studyabroad/florence.ht m

Florida State University
www.international.fsu.edu

Georgetown University
www.villalebalze.org

Gonzaga University
www.gonzaga.edu/studiesabroad/florence.cfm

Harding University
www.harding.edu/international/huf.htm l

James Madison University
www.jmu.edu/international/studyabroad/firenze.
htm l

Kent State University
www.dept.kent.edu/cicp/italy/index.ht m

New York University
www.nyu.edu/global/Florence

Stanford University
www.stanford.firenze.i t

University of Michigan – University of Wisconsin - Duke
www.umich.edu

EUI, European University Institute in Florence
www.iue.it

Richmond, The American University in London -
Florence
www.richmond.ac.uk/undergraduates/special_pro-
grams/florence.as p

Rutgers University
www.studyabroad.rutgers.edu/program_it_flor-
ence_yr.htm l

SCHOOL DAYS

Universities (accredited)

Smith College
www.smith.edu/studyabroad/jya/florence.htm l

Syracuse University
www.syr.fi.it/new/index.htm l

University of Connecticut
www.uconn.edu

California State University
www.calstate.edu

Italian Language Schools

Centro Linguistico Italiano Dante Alighieri
Via Gino Capponi 4
Tel: 055/2478981
www.dantealighieri.it

Scuola Leonardo da Vinci
Via Bufalini 3
Tel: 055/261181
www.scuolaleonardo.com

Linguaviva
Via Fiume 17
Tel: 055/280016
www.linguaviva.it

Eurocentres Firenze
Piazza Santo Spirito 9
Tel: 055/213030
www.ecfi.it

Accademia Europea di Firenze
Via Roma 4
Tel: 055/211599
www.italianlanguageflorence.com

Koinè Center
Via de¹Pandolfini, 27
Tel: 055/213881
www.koinecenter.com

Il Globo
Piazza Santa Maria Novella 22
Tel: 055/2657883
www.ilglobo.it

Machiavelli
Piazza Santo Spirito 4
Tel: 055/2396966
www.centromachiavelli.it

Istituto Il David
Via de' Vecchietti 1
Tel: 055/216110
www.davidschool.com

FLORENCE MUSEUMS, GALLERIES, AND MONUMENTS

Below is a list of the major museums, galleries, and monuments in Florence. In general, museum ticket offices close 40 to 60 minutes before the museum closes. In most cases admission is free for EU citizens under 18 and over 65 and reduced for those aged 18-25.

The list is organized by neighborhoods: 1) Santa Maria Novella, 2) San Giovanni (Duomo), 3) Santa Croce, and 4) Santo Spirito

1) SANTA MARIA NOVELLA

Church of Santa Maria Novella
http://giubileo.comune.fi.it/musei/smnovella/lingue/eng/welcome.html
Some of the most important works of art in Florence, in their original location.
Piazza Santa Maria Novella - Tel. 055 282187
Mon – Thurs & Sat from 9.00 to 17.00; Sundays 9.00 to 14.00
Closed on Fridays
Entrance: € 2,70

Museum of Santa Maria Novella
http://giubileo.comune.fi.it/musei/smnovella/lingue/eng/welcome.html
Piazza Santa Maria Novella - Tel. 055 282187
Mon – Thurs & Sat from 9.00 to 17.00; holidays and Sundays from 9.00 to 14.00
Closed on Fridays
Entrance: € 2,70

Church of Santa Trinita
16th-century façade by Buontalenti and home to Ghirlandaio frescoes.
Piazza Santa Trinita - Tel. 055 216912
Daily from 8.00 to 12.00 and from 16.00 to 18.00
Holidays and Sundays from 16.00 to 18.00
Entrance: Free

Church/Piazza/Cenacolo of Ognissanti

This convent dates from 1251, and the refectory of the convent of Ognissanti is famous for a fresco painted in 1488 by Domenico Ghirlandaio.

Via Borgo Ognissanti 42, 50123 Firenze – Tel. 0552388720

Cenacolo: Mon, Tues, Sat from 9.00 to 12.00

Closed Wed, Thurs, Fri, Sun, and holidays (New Year's Day, May 1st, Christmas Day)

The *Last Supper* can also be visited at other times by prior appointment (055/2396802)

Church: Monday through Saturday, 7.45-12.00 and 16.45 to 18.30

Holidays 7.45-12.00 and 16.45-19.30

Entrance: Free

Marino Marini Museum

http://www.museomarinomarini.it/

Museum dedicated to the great modern Tuscan sculptor.

Piazza Santa Pancrazio - Tel. 055 219432

Mon – Thurs & Sat from 10.00 to 17.00

Closed Tuesday and Sunday

Entrance: € 4,00

2) SAN GIOVANNI (Duomo)

Medici Chapels (Cappelle Medicee)

http://www.firenzemusei.it/00_english/home1.html

This structure houses the Cappella dei Principi (the chapel of the Princes) and the Sagrestia Nuova (New Sacristy) of the San Lorenzo basilica.

Piazza Madonna degli Aldobrandini 6 - Tel. 055 2388602 / for booking: 39 055 294883 fax: 39 055 264406

Daily from 8.15 to 17.00; holidays and Sundays 8.15 to 13.50

Closed on the 2nd and 4th Sunday and the 1st, 3rd, and 5th Monday of every month

Entrance: € 6,00

Accademia Gallery

http://www.firenzemusei.it/00_english/home1.html

Home to the David, the most famous sculpture in the world.

Via Ricasoli 60 - Tel. 055 2388612 / for Booking 39 055 294883
Tues - Sat from 8.15 to 18.50; holidays and Sundays from 8.15 to 18.50
Closed on Mondays
Entrance: € 8,50

Archeology Museum

http://www.firenzemusei.it/00_english/home1.html
One of the most important museums of Etruscan art.
Via della Colonna 38 - Tel. 055 23575
Daily: Mon from 14.00 to 19.00; Tues & Thurs from 8.30 to 19.00; Wed,
Fri & Sat from 8.30 to 14.00
Holidays and Sundays from 8.30 to 14.00
Closed on Christmas, New Years Day, 1st of May
Entrance: € 4,00

Museum of San Marco

http://www.firenzemusei.it/00_english/home1.html
Dedicated to the ethereal paintings of Fra Angelico.
Piazza San Marco 1 - Tel. 055 2388608
Tues - Fri from 8.15 to 13.50; Saturday from 8.15 to 18.50; holidays and
Sundays from 8.15 to 19.00
Closed on Mondays
Entrance: € 4,00

Museo 'Firenze Com'era' / Museum Florence 'As it Was'

Via dell'Oriuolo 24 - Tel. 055 2616545
Mon, Tues, Wed 9.00 to 14.00; Sat 9.00 to 19.00
From June to September: Mon & Tues from 9.00 to 14.00; Saturday
from 9.00 to 19.00
Closed on Thursdays
Entrance: € 2,70

Cathedral of Santa Maria del Fiore

http://www.duomofirenze.it/index-eng.htm
http://www.operaduomo.firenze.it/opera/orari.asp
Piazza Duomo, 9 - Tel. to Cathedral: 055 294514

Daily: Mon, Tues, Weds, Fri from 10.00 to 17.00 / Thur from 10.00 to 16.30
/ 1st Sat of every month, 10.00 to 15.30
Holidays and Sundays from 13.30 to 17.00; special hours New Year's
Day, Easter, Christmas
Entrance: Free

Cupola del Duomo
http://www.duomofirenze.it/index-eng.htm
http://www.operaduomo.firenze.it/opera/orari.asp
This is the dome of the Duomo and the church.
Piazza Duomo - Tel. 055 2302885
Weekdays from 8.30 to 19.00; Saturday from 8.30 to 17.40
Holidays and Sundays: closed
Entrance: € 6,00

Campanile del Duomo
http://www.duomofirenze.it/index-eng.htm
http://www.operaduomo.firenze.it/opera/orari.asp
The Duomo bell tower, designed by Giotto
Piazza Duomo - Tel. 055 2302885
Daily from 8.30 to 19.30
Closed Sundays, January 1, Easter, September 8, Christmas
Entrance: € 6,00

Museo dell'Opera del Duomo/Museum of Works from the Duomo
http://www.duomofirenze.it/index-eng.htm
http://www.operaduomo.firenze.it/opera/orari.asp
The original "Gates of Paradise" are here.
Piazza Duomo 9 - Tel. 055 2302885
Daily from 9.00 to 18.50
Holidays and Sundays from 9.00 to 13.00
Entrance: € 6,00

Palazzo Medici Riccardi / The palace of Cosimo de Medici
http://www.palazzo-medici.it/eng/home.htm
Via Cavour 3 - Tel. 055 2760340
Mon & Tues, Thurs–Sat from 9.00 to 19.00

Holidays and Sundays from 9.00 to 19.00
Closed on Wednesday
Entrance: € 5,00

Ospedale degli Innocenti / Hospital of the Innocents
http://www.istitutodeglinnocenti.it/index.jsf
The world's first orphanage.
Piazza SS. Annunziata 12 – Tel. 055 2037308
Tel.055 2491708
The gallery is open daily from 8.30 to 14.00
Closed on Wednesday
Entrance: € 4,00

Stibbert Museum
http://www.museostibbert.it/index.htm
Bizarre and vast arms collection
Via Stibbert 26 - Tel. 055 475520
Mon, Tues, Wed from 10.00 to 14.00; Fri, Sat, Sun from 10.00 to 18.00
Closed on Thursday
Entrance: € 6,00

Baptistery of San Giovanni
http://www.operaduomo.firenze.it/english/#
Next to the Duomo (with exterior doors called 'The Gates of Paradise')
Piazza S. Giovanni - Tel. 055 2302885
Daily from 12.00 to 19.00
Holidays and Sundays from 8.30 to 14.00
Closed January 1, Easter, September 8, December 24, Christmas
Entrance: € 3,00

Chiesa e Museo di Orsanmichele / Church and Museum of Orsanmichele
From grain storage to church.
Via Arte della Lana - Tel. 055 284944
Daily from 9.00 to 12.00 and from 16.00 to 18.00
Closed 1st and last Monday of every month
Entrance: Free

Church of San Lorenzo
Church with a rough façade and incredible interior.
Piazza San Lorenzo - Tel. 055 216634 / 055 218534
Daily from 10.00 to 17.00
Closed Holidays and Sundays
Entrance: € 2,58

Church of Santissima Annunziata
Heavily ornamented, and perhaps more typical church of Italy.
Piazza SS. Annunziata - Tel. 055 2398034
Daily from 7.30 to 12.30 and from 16.00 to 18.30
Holidays and Sundays from 7.30 to 12.30 and from 16.00 to 18.30
Entrance: Free

Opificio delle Pietre Dure
http://www.opificio.arti.beniculturali.it/eng/index.htm
Laboratory of semi-precious stones.
Via Alfani, 78 - Tel: 055 26511
Mon-Sat 8:15-14:00; Thursday 8:15-19:00
Closed Sunday and holidays
Entrance: € 2,00

3) SANTA CROCE

Cenacolo di San Salvi / Monastery of San Salvi
Home of famous Renaissance Last Supper fresco by Andrea del Sarto
Via di S. Salvi 16 - Tel. 055 2388603
Daily from 8.15 to 13.50
Holidays and Sundays from 8.15 to 13.50
Closed on Monday
Entrance: Free

Uffizi Gallery
http://www.polomuseale.firenze.it/english/musei/uffizi/Default.asp
The Uffizi Gallery is one of the greatest museums in Italy and the world and contains masterpieces by artists such as Giotto, Leonardo da Vinci, Botticelli, Michelangelo, and many others.

Piazza Uffizi 6 - Tel. 055 2388651 / For Booking: 055 294883
Tues - Sun, from 8.15 to 18.50
Holidays and Sundays from 8.15 to 18.50
Closed on Mondays, New Year's Day, May 1st and Christmas Day
Entrance: € 6,50

Bargello Museum
http://www.firenzemusei.it/00_english/home1.html
Once a prison, now home to some of Italy's finest sculpture.
Via del Proconsolo 4 - Tel. 055 2388606 / For Booking information:
055 294883
Daily from 8.15 to 14.00
Holidays and Sundays from 8.15 to 14.00
Closed on New Year's Day, May 1st and Christmas Day
Entrance: € 4,00

Palazzo Vecchio
Modern-day home of town hall for Florence, next to Uffizi.
Piazza Signoria - Tel. 055 2768465
Mon – Weds, Fri & Sat from 9.00 to 19.00; Thursday from 9.00 to 14.00
Holidays and Sundays from 9.00 to 19.00
Entrance: € 6,00

Casa Buonarroti
http://www.casabuonarroti.it/
Dedicated to Michelangelo.
Via Ghibellina 70 - Tel. 055 241752
Mon, Weds - Sat, from 9.30 to 14.00
During temporary exhibitions, 9.30-16.00
Holidays and Sundays from 9.30 to 16.00
Closed on Tuesdays and January 1, Easter Sunday, May 1st, August
15th, December 25th.
Entrance: € 6,50

Museo della Fondazione Horne/Horne Museum
Restored Renaissance palazzo and art collection of Herbert P. Horne.
Via dei Benci 6 - Tel. 055 244661

Monday through Saturday, from 9.00 to 13.00
Holidays and Sundays: Closed
June—September: Open Tuesday evenings 20.30-23.00
Entrance: € 5,00

Istituto e Museo di Storia della Scienza/Museum of the History of Science

This museum shows that Florence was a center of scientific research. Holds some of Galileo's original experiments.
Piazza dei Giudici 1 - Tel. 055 265311
Summer (June 1 - September 30): Mon, Weds, Thurs & Fri from 9.30 to 17.00; Tues and Sat from 9.30 to 13.00
Evening (21.00 to 23.30): last Thursday of June and August; first Thursday of July and September
Closed on Sundays and holidays
Winter (October 1 - May 31): Mon, Weds, Thurs – Sat from 9.30 to 17.00; Tues from 9.30 to 13.00
Closed on Sundays except the second Sunday of each month 10.00 to 13.00
Entrance: € 6,50

Church of Santa Croce

Includes monuments to Dante, Michelangelo, and others.
Piazza Santa Croce - Tel. 055 244619
Daily: Summer from 9.30 to 17.30 Winter from 8.00 to 12.30 and 15.00 to 17.30
Holidays and Sundays from 13.00 to 17.30
Entrance: € 3,00 (includes museum)

Museum of the works of Santa Croce

(Access is through the church.)
Piazza S. Croce 16 - Tel. 055 244619
Mon - Sat from 9.30 to 17.30
Holidays and Sundays from 13.00 to 17.30
Entrance: € 3,00

4) SANTO SPIRITO

Palazzo Pitti / Pitti Palace

http://www.palazzopitti.it/

This palace, originally commissioned in 1448, is now home to various museums and the Boboli Gardens.

Tuesday to Sunday, from 8.30 to 19.00

Piazza Pitti 1 Tel. 055 212688 or for booking: 055 294 883

Entrance: Pitti Palace inclusive ticket (valid 3 days) includes the entire museum complex of the Pitti Palace. Full price: € 11.50; Reduced price: € 5.75.

Entry after 4 pm: full price € 9.00; reduced price € 4.50.

The inclusive ticket is not available when exhibitions are being held in any of the museums.

The booking service is available at the two information desks in the Pitti Palace and in the reception area of the New Uffizi, and via a telephone booking centre. The information and booking desks are open during the museum opening times (Tuesday to Sunday, from 8.30 to 19.00); the telephone booking centre (+39 (0)55 294883) is open from Monday to Friday from 8.30 to 18.30 and on Saturdays from 8.30 to 12.30.

Visiting either of the two information desks or phoning the booking centre, you will receive free information on opening times, exhibitions, admission charges and can also book a visit to any of the Firenze Musei museums. (There is a booking and advance sales charge of Euro 3.00. Booking will only be considered confirmed after payment has taken place.)

Boboli Gardens

http://www.firenzemusei.it/00_english/home1.html

Just behind Palazzo Pitti, extends one of the largest and most beautiful examples of the Italian garden.

Tel. 055 2388786 / Booking: 055 294883

Daily. November - February: 8.15-16.30; March: 8.15-17.30; April & May, September & October: 8:15-19.30 20; June, July, August 8:15-19:30

Closed: first and last Monday of month, holidays

Entrance: € 3,00 / € 6.00, booking (optional); 50% reduction for 18-25 year olds from the European Union and for regular state teachers.

Modern Art Gallery

http://www.firenzemusei.it/00_english/home1.html
The gallery, located on the second floor of the Palazzo Pitti, primarily has paintings from the 18th and 19th centuries.
Piazza Pitti - Tel. 055 2388601/616
Tuesday-Sunday: 8.15-18.50
Closed on Mondays, New Year's Day, May 1st and Christmas Day
Entrance: Palatine Gallery and the Gallery of Modern Art: € 8.50
Booking (optional): € 3.00; 50% reduction for 18-25 year olds from the European Union and for regular state teachers.

Gallery of Costumes

http://www.firenzemusei.it/00_english/moderna/index.html
This is one of the several galleries within the walls of the Pitti Palace.
Piazza Pitti - Tel. 055 2388601/616
Tuesday-Sunday: 8.15-18.50
Closed on Mondays, New Year's Day, May 1st and Christmas Day
Entrance: Palatine Gallery and the Gallery of Modern Art: € 8.50
Booking (optional): € 3.00; 50% reduction for 18-25 year olds from the European Union and for regular state teachers.

Palatina Gallery and Royal Apartments

http://www.firenzemusei.it/00_english/palatina/index.html
This Pitti Palace gallery has an important collection of paintings from the 15th to 17th century.
Piazza Pitti - Tel. 055 2388614 / Booking: 055 294883
Tuesday - Sunday: from 8.15 to 18.50
Closed on Mondays, New Year's Day, May 1st, Christmas Day. The Royal Apartments are closed for maintenance every year in January.
Entrance: Palatine Gallery and the Gallery of Modern Art: € 8.50, booking (optional): € 3.00; 50% reduction for 18-25 year olds from the European Union and for regular state teachers.

Museum of Silver

There is much more than silver in this impressive museum.
Piazza Pitti - Tel. 055 2388709-761
November to February, from 8.15 to 16.30

March: 8.15 to 17.30
April & May, September & October: 8.15 to 18.30
October (after daylight saving ends): 8.15 to 17.30
June, July, August: 8.15 to 19.30
Closed December 25th, January 1st, May 1st
Entrance: € 2,00 or buy an all-inclusive ticket at the ticket office at the Pitti Palace.

Museum of Porcelain
This museum contains ceramics from factories of Sevre, Meissen and Vienna.
Giardino di Boboli/Boboli Garden Tel. 055 2388709
November to February from 8.15 to 16.30
March: 8.15 to 17.30
April & May, September & October: 8.15 to 18.30
October (after daylight saving ends): 8.15 to 17.30
June, July, August: 8.15 to 19.30
Entrance: € 3,00 or buy an all-inclusive ticket at the ticket office of the Pitti Palace

Brancacci Chapel
Known for 15th-century frescoes by Masaccio and Masolino; see the film as well.
Timed tickets only.
Piazza del Carmine 14 - Tel. 055 2382195
Mon, Weds - Sat from 10.00 to 17.00
Holidays and Sundays from 13.00 to 17.00
Closed on Tuesdays
Entrance: € 3,10

Zoological Museum La Specola
http://www.specola.unifi.it
Opened in 1775 by Grand Duke Pietro Leopoldo of Lorraine and claims to be the oldest scientific museum in Europe.
Via Romana 17 - Tel. 055 228825
Mon, Tues, Thurs - Sat from 9.00 to 13.00
Holidays and Sundays from 9.00 to 13.00

Closed on Wednesday
Entrance: € 5,00

Church of San Miniato al Monte
Beautiful marble façade and an exceptional interior.
Via Monte alle Croci - Tel. 055 2342731
Summer: daily from 8.00 to 12.30 and 14.30 to 19.30
Winter: daily from 8.00 to 19.30
Entrance: Free

Church of San Spirito
Some say this church was Brunellieschi's greatest work.
Piazza Santo Spirito - Tel. 055 210030
Daily from 8.30 to 12.00 and from 16.00 to 18.30
Holidays and Sundays from 16.00 to 18.30
Closed on Wednesday afternoons
Entrance: Free

Cenacolo of Santo Spirito
Former Augustian refectory.
Piazza Santo Spirito 29 - Tel. 055 287043
Tuesday - Saturday from 9.00 to 14.00
Holidays and Sundays from 9.00 to 14.00
Closed on Mondays
Entrance: € 2,10

Forte di Belvedere
This fort has one of the most beautiful views of Florence and is host to important modern art exhibitions.
Via S. Leonardo - Tel. 055 2001486
Winter: daily 9 -18
Summer: daily 9 - 19
(hours may vary for exhibitions)
Entrance: € 8,00

Italian Embassies and Consulates in Anglophone Countries

Australia
Embassy of Italy in Canberra, Australia
12, Grey Street
Phone: 612/627 33333
Fax: 612/62734223
http://www.ambitalia.org.au
embassy@ambitalia.org.au

Canada
Embassy of Italy in Ottawa, Canada
275, Slater Street- 21st floor
Ottawa. Canada
Phone: 16/132322401
Fax: 16/132331484
http://www.italyincanada.com
ambital@italyincanada.com

Italian Consulate in Edmonton
1900, Royal Trust Tower
Edmonton Centre, Alberta
consitedm@compusmart.ab.ca

Italian Consulate in Hamilton
105, Main Street East - Suite 509
Hamilton, Ontario
Phone: 905/5295030
Fax: 905/5297028

Italian Consulate in Montreal
3489, Drummond Street
Montreal, Quebec
Phone: 514/8498351
Fax: 514/4999471
cgi@italconsul.montreal.qc.ca

Italian Consulate In Toronto
136, Beverley Street
Toronto, Ontario
Phone: 416/9771566,
Fax: 416/977119

Italian Consulate in Vancouver
1100-510 West Hastings Street
Vancouver B.C
Phone: 604/6847212
Fax: 604/6854263
italcons@axion.net

Great Britain

Embassy of Italy in London, England (UK)
14, Three Kings Yard
London W1K 4EH
Phone: (0) 20/73122200
Fax: (0) 20/73122230
http://www.amblondra.esteri.it
ambasciata.londra@esteri.it

Consulate General of Italy in London, England (UK)
38 Eaton Place
London SW1X 8AN
Phone: 0044-20/7235 9371
Fax: 0044-20 78231609
consolato.londra@esteri.it

United States

Embassy of Italy Washington DC, United States
3000 Whitehaven Street
NW Washington DC 20008

United States
Phone: 12/02612 4400
Fax: 12/025182151
http://www.ambwashingtondc.esteri.it/Ambasciata_Washington/
visti.washington@esteri.it

Consulate General of Italy in Boston, United States

600 Atlantic Avenue 17th floor
Boston, MA 02210
United States
Phone: +1 (617) 722-9201/02/03
Fax: +1 (617) 722-9407
http://www.consboston.esteri.it/Consolato_Boston
archivio.boston@esteri.it

Consulate General of Italy in Chicago, United States

500 North Michigan Avenue,
suite 1850
Chicago IL 60611
United States
Phone: (312) 467-1550/1/2
Fax: (312) 467-1335
http://www.conschicago.esteri.it/Consolato_Chicago
italcons.chicago@esteri.it

Consulate General of Italy in Detroit, United States

535 Griswold - Buhl Building,
Suite 1840
Detroit, Michigan
Phone: (313) 963-8560
Fax: (313) 963-8180
http://www.consdetroit.esteri.it/Consolato_Detroit
inform.detroit@esteri.it

Consulate General of Italy in Philadelphia, United States

1026 Public Ledger Building
150 South Independence Mall West

Philadelphia, PA 19106
Phone: 215 592 7329
Fax: 215 592 9808
http://www.consfiladelfia.esteri.it/Consolato_Filadelfia
consolato.filadelfia@esteri.it

Consulate General of Italy in Houston, United States
1300 Post Oak Boulevard - Suite 660
Houston, Texas 77056
Phone: 713/8507520
Fax: 713/8509113
http://www.conshouston.esteri.it/Consolato_Houston
italcons.houston@esteri.it

Consulate General of Italy in Los Angeles, United States
12400 Wilshire Blvd.
300 (Between Bundy & Centinela)
Los Angeles, Calif. 90025
Phone: (310) 820-0622
Fax: (310) 820-0727
http://www.conslosangeles.esteri.it/Consolato_LosAngeles
consolato.losangeles@esteri.it

Consulate General of Italy in Miami, United States
4000 Ponce de Leon
Suite 590
Coral Gables, FL 33146
Phone: +1-305-374-6322
Fax: +1-305-374-7945
http://www.consmiami.esteri.it/Consolato_Miami
italianconsulate.miami@esteri.it

OTHER EMBASSIES CONSULATES WORLDWIDE:
Check website: www.embassiesabroad.com

Foreign Anglophone Consulates in Florence

Consulate General of the United States
Lungarno Vespucci, 38
50123 Firenze, Italy
Phone. (+39) 055/266951
Fax (+39) 055.284.088
Website: www.florence.usconsulate.gov

British Consulate of Florence
Lungarno Corsini 2
50123 Firenze
Phone: 055/284133
Consular.florence@fco.gov.uk

Anglophone Embassies in Rome

Australian Embassy – Rome
Via Antonio Bosio, 5
1-00817 Rome
Phone: 06 852 721
Fax: 06 8522300
www.italy.embassy.gov.au

British Embassy – Rome
Via XX Settembre 80
1 – 00187 Roma
Phone: 06/42200001
www.britishembassy.gov.uk

Canadian Embassy - Rome

Via Zara 30 - Rome, Italy 00198
Phone: + (39) 06/854441
Fax: + (39) 06/854442912

Embassy of the United States of America

Via Vittorio Veneto 121
00187 Rome
UScitizensRome@state.gov
www.RomeUSembassy.gov

46126784R00123

Made in the USA
San Bernardino, CA
26 February 2017